Developments in Handwriting and Signature Identification in the Digital Age

Developments in Handwriting and Signature Identification in the Digital Age

Heidi H. Harralson

Series Editor
Larry S. Miller

AMSTERDAM • BOSTON • HEIDELBERG • LONDON
NEW YORK • OXFORD • PARIS • SAN DIEGO
SAN FRANCISCO • SINGAPORE • SYDNEY • TOKYO
Anderson Publishing is an imprint of Elsevier

Anderson Publishing is an imprint of Elsevier
The Boulevard, Langford Lane, Kidlington, Oxford, OX5 1GB, UK
225 Wyman Street, Waltham, MA 02451, USA

First published 2013

Notices
Knowledge and best practice in this field are constantly changing. As new research and experience
broaden our understanding, changes in research methods, professional practices, or medical treatment
may become necessary.

Practitioners and researchers must always rely on their own experience and knowledge in evaluating
and using any information, methods, compounds, or experiments described herein. In using such
information or methods they should be mindful of their own safety and the safety of others, including
parties for whom they have a professional responsibility.

To the fullest extent of the law, neither the Publisher nor the authors, contributors, or editors, assume
any liability for any injury and/or damage to persons or property as a matter of products liability,
negligence or otherwise, or from any use or operation of any methods, products, instructions, or ideas
contained in the material herein.

British Library Cataloguing in Publication Data
A catalogue record for this book is available from the British Library

Library of Congress Cataloging-in-Publication Data
A catalog record for this book is available from the Library of Congress

ISBN: 978-1-45-573147-3

For information on all Anderson Publishing
publications visit our website at **store.elsevier.com**

This book has been manufactured using Print On Demand technology. Each copy is produced to
order and is limited to black ink. The online version of this book will show color figures where
appropriate.

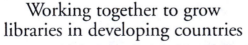

Working together to grow
libraries in developing countries

www.elsevier.com | www.bookaid.org | www.sabre.org

ELSEVIER   **BOOK AID**
International   **Sabre Foundation**

Transferred to Digital Printing in 2012

TABLE OF CONTENTS

PREFACE

This book is part of a series published by Elsevier on specialized forensic topics. Because of its smaller, more focused subject matter, the format is ideally suited for updating our current knowledge of forensic handwriting identification.

The analysis of electronic signatures is an ever-growing trend requiring specialized research and new methodology by forensic practitioners. This text hopes to give some focus in this new area by defining misunderstood terms, identifying problems and challenges to forensic handwriting identification, and recommending methods of practice.

This book is the result of research that initiated at Prescott College in Arizona focusing on medical motor disorders and forgery. During my research work at Prescott College and the University of Arizona, I was introduced to handwriting movement software and the digital tablet. I would have continued my work on handwriting and motor disorders, but during a visit at the Norwegian Information Security Lab (NISlab) in Gjøvik, I was encouraged by professors at the laboratory to pursue research into the forensic study of electronic signatures. I consider this book a synthesis of my research work over the years at several different universities.

First, I want to thank Katrin Franke at NISlab in Gjøvik, Norway for initiating my interest in electronic signatures. I am grateful for the dedicated research work carried out by Bryan Found and Doug Rogers and their students, especially since much of their research is cited in this book. Many of the more recent concepts concerning handwriting identification theory have been developed by researchers at LaTrobe University in Australia.

I especially thank Hans-Leo Teulings, developer of MovAlyzeR movement analysis software system at NeuroScript, LLC. He has been an instructor, editor, and coauthor in many of my research publications and provided technical assistance in several of the chapters in this book. Without his years of expertise and generous assistance, I would not have been able to bridge the gap between the technical aspects of electronically captured handwriting movement and its practical application in forensic science.

Finally, I extend appreciation to Larry Miller at East Tennessee State University, Department of Criminal Justice and Criminology. He is not only the editor of this book but has also been my mentor and research partner for many years. I am indebted to him not only for his inspirational research work on forensic bias and the technical aspects of forensic science, but also for inspiring me to academically challenge myself in the forensic field.

Research in electronic signatures is growing and the developing technology is taking several different directions. In a short period of time, this book will need to be revised to keep up with the latest research and technological innovations. I am looking forward to a future edition where I will have the opportunity to update the concepts in this emerging field.

Heidi H. Harralson

CHAPTER 1

Introduction

1.1 KEY CONCEPTS IN FORENSIC HANDWRITING EXAMINATION
1.2 FORGERY AND SIMULATION

The purpose of this text is not to rewrite or even summarize all of the document examination literature that has been written since the early part of the twentieth century. Rather, the goal is to summarize and discuss the pertinent research and literature that represents significant development in bringing handwriting and signature identification into the digital age as well as the challenges presented in merging handwriting with digital technology. Some of the subject matter may seem to have little to do with digital technology, such as sections that discuss children's handwriting training and development; yet this is an important topic as it establishes how handwriting is changing culturally (which has implications in the way handwriting experts examine handwriting), and how those changes may be by-products of the digital age in which we live.

Other books and published articles extensively discuss the process of forensic handwriting examination. Some of the classic texts such as Albert Osborn's (1929) seminal work "Questioned Documents" include discussions about class characteristics of penmanship systems (such as the Palmer Method). More recent works such as Seaman Kelly & Lindblom's (2006) text "Scientific Examination of Questioned Documents" (a revision of an older work by Ordway Hilton) discusses advances in technical areas such as identification of print process methods and analyzing computer-generated documents. While much of the material, even in older, classic works is relevant, it is important to update our collective knowledge in this specialized area as the way we write today and even the way in which we analyze handwriting scientifically has undergone fundamental changes. Research across several disciplines in computer science, medicine, neurology, and engineering has reshaped what we know about handwriting and contributed to new methods in its forensic analysis and identification.

Significant strides have been made in the scientific and legal acceptance of forensic handwriting identification. Proficiency studies on forensic handwriting experts' accuracy rates in addition to empirical studies on the individuality of handwriting have helped to establish the field's scientific acceptance. This acceptance has not come easily especially since handwriting identification was one of the first forensic disciplines to come under criticism by the legal and scientific communities.

Additionally, court rulings have also helped solidify the field's acceptance in rulings such as the recent *Pettus v. United States* case in the District of Columbia Court of Appeals (2012). During trial, it was challenged that handwriting identification does not meet the trial court's test of general acceptance of a particular scientific methodology. The challenge was supported by statements made by a report commissioned by Congress and published by the National Research Council of the National Academies of Science (2009) that criticizes pattern-based forensic evidence. However, the Court ruled that forensic handwriting examination satisfied the bedrock admissibility standard of *Frye v. United States* (1923), and the forensic document examiner's testimony was admitted.

In defending the field's scientific acceptance during court testimony, the document examiner cited many of the principles relied on by document examiners in the field. Rather than rewrite the accepted principles in questioned document literature, some of these principles will be discussed as needed in the various chapters under discussion, but some significant points are also discussed at the end of this section so that the reader will have a basic introduction to the subject. These points are summarized briefly for the reader in order to allow adequate digestion of information about forensic handwriting identification and point the reader to texts that delve deeper into these accepted and generally recognized principles.

The subject matter of this text all relates to handwriting examination, but it is a collection of research from different disciplines that can provide knowledge useful to updating our knowledge of forensic handwriting identification. Chapter 2 is a discussion about cultural changes in handwriting, initially discussing its purported "death" as reported in the media. Handwriting is not dead insomuch as it is transitioning with the advances of digital technology. The deterioration of handwriting is a product of both decreased classroom training and the increased use of text-based technological devices. Why handwriting training is decreasing, reasons why handwriting is important to the developing brain, and ways in which teachers can introduce handwriting training to students is discussed. How the cultural changes in handwriting affect its forensic examination is reviewed including areas such as learning disabilities (which are increasing in the population), and how illegible or poorly formed handwriting and signatures have challenged handwriting identification. New methods introduced to the handwriting identification field may have resulted due to the occurrence of overly simplified signature styles which can present forensic examination challenges.

Significant advances have been made in understanding the connection between the brain and handwriting. Their resulting disorder as manifested in handwriting movement is the subject of Chapter 3. Much of this research has been developed with the aid of electronic technology by analyzing static features as well as the online, biometric movements of the tablet pen with handwriting movement captured by electronic handwriting recording software. The electronic capture of handwriting movement has revolutionized what we know about handwriting movement with much of the research originating from the medical and handwriting recognition fields. Handwriting movement research that has forensic relevance is reviewed for various health and psychiatric conditions in handwriting including related medications, the influence of alcohol in handwriting, specific forensic applications such as simulation or forgery, disguise, and other neuro-technological advances in handwriting sciences.

Electronic handwriting is introduced in Chapter 4, which defines different types of digital and electronic signatures. Much of the technology discussed in this chapter was introduced in Chapter 3 but is explored in greater detail through the hardware and software used in electronic signature technology. Different types of digital tablets, styluses and unusual "pens," and other unusual methods used to capture electronic signatures are described and evaluated for their forensic relevance and the possible challenges they may present in handwriting identification. The digitization process of signatures is reviewed as well as an overview of handwriting recognition technology and the advent of automated forensic handwriting analysis.

The heart of the subject, Chapter 5, involves the forensic examination of digital and electronic signatures and handwriting. After introducing the types of electronic-capturing devices and methods employed in Chapter 4, Chapter 5 examines their use in relation to forensic examination and challenges associated with electronic interpretation of signatures from both a hardware and software perspective, the variables involved with the way signers approach electronic devices, and how devices change natural handwriting. The diverse technology used for signature capture including poor and high-quality resolution capture presents challenges in forensic analysis. The need for standardization in electronic signature examination is obviously needed, but until that is realized, if ever, it is recognized that forensic examiners may need to approach these types of signatures conservatively. Recommended methods and standards for the forensic examination of electronic signatures are introduced. A recent court case involving a disputed electronic signature is reviewed as it highlights the challenges facing document examiners in the courtroom when examining and testifying in electronic signature cases.

Lastly, Chapter 6 examines recent developments in the scientific acceptance of handwriting as well as legal rulings and precedence concerning the legal acceptance of forensic handwriting identification. Starting with the challenges presented by a recent government report's challenge to forensic science, an overview of how handwriting identification has successfully met scientific and legal challenges is presented through accreditation, proficiency testing, scientific validity and reliability research, standardization of terminology and methodology, and advances in computerized handwriting analysis.

A glossary is provided at the end of the text to assist the reader with highly technical terms related to digital and electronic signatures. The glossary is also provided to help with defining terms in the field as there is some confusion about what exactly a digital signature is, especially since it is a broad term covering several different "signature" modalities.

1.1 KEY CONCEPTS IN FORENSIC HANDWRITING EXAMINATION

In order for the reader to have adequate understanding of forensic handwriting examination, this introduction will serve as a summary to some of the most important principles recognized by document examiners. These key concepts will help the reader understand the principles of forensic handwriting identification.

One of the most important principles involves the handwriting variation of a single writer. It is a generally accepted handwriting principle

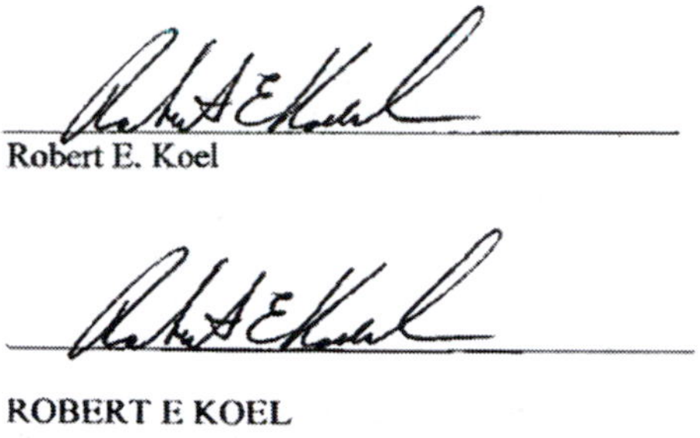

Fig. 1.1 Example of two identical signatures indicative that one is a "cut-and-paste" signature.

that no two handwritings or signatures are written exactly alike by the same person. If a handwriting expert finds an identical signature to the one that is being questioned, it is an indicator that one may be a copy of the other which may be based on a tracing, a copy, or a scan of one signature that is placed on another document (Fig. 1.1).

It is generally accepted that handwriting has a combination of features that are unique and identifiable for each writer. It is believed that not only are no two signatures written exactly alike by one person, but that no other person writes all the same features in the same way as another writer. This principle is also based on the examination of multiple handwriting features as this could not be supported if the examiner relied upon one or two handwriting features. Handwriting is not only unique but its various features are interrelated, creating a complex handwriting formula for each individual writer.

The principle that no two handwritings are written exactly alike is related to the concept that each writer has a natural range of variation. As such, handwriting is pattern based and rather than relying on isolated handwriting features, handwriting experts examine patterns in handwriting. In order to establish range of variation for a writer, the pattern needs to be established in a number of comparison samples. Rarely can an identification or elimination of a handwriting or signature be accomplished with one or even a few handwriting comparison samples. So, due to natural range of variation, multiple handwriting or signature samples are necessary in the examination. Because handwriting is not static and is subject to change over time or due to other variable conditions, handwriting samples written during a comparable time period and under the same conditions applying to the questioned writing material are also necessary (Fig. 1.2).

Fig. 1.2 Three signatures written by the same person in a sequence. Note the natural variation between the signatures.

This naturally leads to the next point involving natural and unnatural handwriting. One of the first steps in a handwriting examination involves the assessment of the handwriting samples under inspection. The examiner needs to evaluate the samples and determine if they possess the characteristics of natural handwriting. Natural handwriting has an unimpeded flow of movement. Handwriting can be affected by adverse factors such as health, external circumstances, medications, alcohol, and other conditions. If the subject writing exhibits extraordinary characteristics or dysfluency, the examiner needs to determine if it can be compared to other samples that do exhibit natural characteristics and/ or make a determination as to why the unnatural handwriting characteristics are occurring (which could also be related to forgery or simulation).

Document examiners rely on methodological standards to standardize their examination procedures. One method that has been extensively used is Analyze, Compare, and Evaluate (ACE). This method is used in the standard developed for handwriting examination published by the American Standards for Testing and Materials International, E2290-07a (2007). Other methodological standards have been published in forensic document examination literature and include rating scales and modular approaches (Found & Rogers, 1999; Slyter, 1995). The Scientific Working Group for Forensic Document Examination (SWGDOC) is administered by the Federal Bureau of Investigation (FBI) and the U.S. Department of Justice and publishes standards for government document examiners.

1.2 FORGERY AND SIMULATION

Technically, the widely used term "forgery" is a legal term which refers (for the purposes of handwriting identification) not only to the imitation of a handwriting or signature but also to the intent on the part of the forger to defraud. So, only part of the term "forgery" is relevant to a forensic handwriting expert as the intent of the signer with regard to the instrument that is being written or signed is beyond the scope of service for the forensic expert. In court, the forensic expert would refer to what is popularly referred to as "forgery" as "simulation" of the handwriting form. Determining intent is the prerogative of the trier of fact. For purposes of clarity, the more popular term "forgery" will be used interchangeably with "simulation" in this text.

Different forgery methods have been identified and are included here for general reference. There is more than one way to forge a signature and some forgers are more skilled at imitating signatures than others. Additionally, not all forgeries may be detectable with the unaided eye. The following are common methods used to forge signatures.

With the simple spurious type, the forger does not have access to a model of the genuine writer's signature. As a result, there is no attempt to imitate the genuine writer's signature. This type of forgery frequently occurs in stolen check cases because the genuine writer's signature is not available to the forger.

Freehand simulation occurs when the forger copies from a model by looking at the signature and attempts to imitate the form or general style of the signature. The forger may practice the signature several times before writing it on the fraudulent document. Depending on the writer, these types of forgeries demonstrate varying degrees of skill. However, an unskilled writer is not able to successfully imitate a skilled signature.

In tracing, the forger copies the signature by placing the fraudulent document on top of a genuine signature. A backlight or light box may be used in order to see the genuine signature more clearly. Carbon paper and pencil rubbing may also be used in traced forgeries. The carbon or pencil tracings may be visible with infrared and/or magnification (Fig. 1.3). The tracing method can also be used in electronic signature technology.

Transfer forgery occurs when a copy of a genuine signature is transferred onto another document. This can be done by photocopying the genuine signature and placing it onto the target document and then photocopying the newly created document so that the signature appears to be a natural part of the document. In such cases, original questioned documents do not exist. Alternatively, a signature may be scanned, digitally transferred onto another document, and then printed. These types of signatures can be hard to detect with the

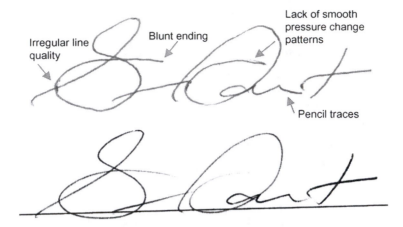

Fig. 1.3 A forged signature created by tracing (top). Note the unnatural line quality and slowness of execution compared to the authentic model signature (bottom).

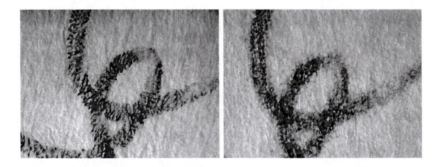

Fig. 1.4 Microscopic comparison of an original ink signature (left) and a computer-generated copy of the same signature printed on a color ink-jet printer (right). Notice the multicolored dots in the image on the right.

unaided eye because, using computer techniques, the signature can be colored and manipulated in such a way that it looks like original ink. Because no two signatures by a genuine writer are exactly alike, the discovery of two identical signatures on different documents indicates that one of the signatures has been copied and transferred (Fig. 1.4).

For a comprehensive review, the reader can find more information about forensic handwriting and document examination topics in several texts which are listed in the reference section in this book and which include Caligiuri & Mohammed (2012), Conway (1959), Ellen (2006), Found & Rogers (1999), Harrison (1958), Hilton (1993), Huber & Headrick (1999), Osborn (1929), Seaman Kelly & Lindblom (2006), and Slyter (1995).

CHAPTER 2

The Decline of Handwriting

2.1   THE NEED FOR HANDWRITING INSTRUCTION

2.2   THE IMPORTANCE OF HANDWRITING

2.3   HANDWRITING INSTRUCTION METHODS

2.4   INFLUENCE OF LEARNING DISABILITIES ON HANDWRITING

2.5   FORENSIC PROBLEMS WITH ILLEGIBLE AND PRINTED HANDWRITING

2.6   SUMMARY

A 14-year-old adolescent, while listening to "Suicide Hotline" by *Insane Clown Posse* heavy metal rap band on his iPod, pens his last words in a suicide note, scrawling his large printing with a pencil on wide-ruled paper from a spiral binder. Having never learned cursive, his handprinting looks awkward and misspelled, lacking the maturity of the cursive on which his great-grandparents so prided themselves. His handwriting's poor arrangement, and its confused use of uppercase letters in the middle of printed words, would suggest to a handwriting researcher that the youth may have learning disorders. His writing consistency is also affected by his abuse of illegal substances combined with prescription medications for attention deficit disorder (ADD). The youth writes several passages from the Biblical text Ecclesiastes onto his lined notepaper. After he finishes the last verse, "Who can tell him what will happen under the sun after he is gone?", he puts his pencil down and picks up the handgun laying beside him. He raises the muzzle of the gun to his head and pulls the trigger.

A tale of teen suicide is admittedly an unusual way to begin a book with a focus on electronic handwriting. However, it is an appropriate beginning for a book on handwriting in the digital age, because the changes in handwriting that have occurred over the past few decades are closely linked to the fact that our handwriting, collectively, has been changed by the advent of computer technology. Technology has contributed to the way we write both in terms of handwriting and linguistic style. Printing is much more prevalent now than it was several decades ago. As a result of e-mail and texting, we have created new "words" and abbreviations that are not part of our formal language. We are spending less time in the classroom teaching children how to write properly which, in turn, is collectively influencing the writing style that is used for producing handwritten text. These are important concerns that forensic document examiners need to address, because changes in handwriting require new approaches to the way we examine handwriting, and not just in cases involving electronic signatures.

The teen suicide note introduced in the case above was submitted to a forensic document examiner for handwriting identification (Harralson, 2007–2008). Such cases underscore the need by handwriting experts to update methods that are affected by cultural changes in handwriting as well as the influence of handwriting training methods on school-age youth. Many of the classic texts on handwriting identification are based upon identification of class characteristics which are derived from penmanship models such as the Palmer and Zaner–Bloser methods. While these models are still taught in some schools, they do not have the widespread popularity that they did decades ago, nor are these methods instilled into students with the same level of rigor. Fluency in handwriting is one of the signs of natural handwriting that is used to compare to forged handwriting, which is frequently lacking in fluent writing features. Instead, forged writing exhibits characteristics of someone who does not know how to write: slowly drawn as though the writer were copying from a model. Learning disabilities further affect handwriting because they decrease fluency and increase the writer's natural range of variation, factors that influence forensic handwriting examination.

The teen suicide case, previously mentioned, was written from the perspective of the defendant, his twin brother. The prosecution purported that the youth had been shot by his twin brother. Both brothers were identical twins, aged 14, who were further described as mirror twins (e.g., one twin was left-handed and the other right-handed). The twin brothers were enrolled in middle school, but both were at least one year behind their cohort age group. Because they had not been intensively trained in a cursive copybook system, this could have increased the level of individual characteristics in their handwriting. Limited handwriting training could correspondingly have increased variability

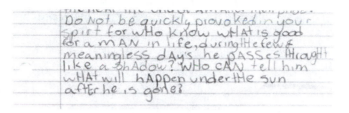

Fig. 2.1 Part of handwritten note found at crime scene of alleged teen suicide case.

in their writing (evident in the adolescents' known handwriting samples) since they had not been taught a handwriting system intensively to allow for development of graphic maturity. Further, the twins sometimes wrote in a gang style script and the right-handed twin seemed to imitate his brother's style in at least one sample. The twins had learning disabilities including ADD. They had been prescribed Ritalin and psychotropic medications for both learning disabilities and psychological problems. They had a history of juvenile delinquency that included taking illegal drugs and alcohol. The combination of these factors affected the consistency and fluency of the handwriting samples examined in the case (Fig. 2.1).

The left-handed twin died from a fatal gunshot wound to the head. The prosecution charged his brother with manslaughter while the defense contended that he committed suicide. The disputed documents involved an alleged suicide note and entries from a notebook expressing what were considered "suicidal ideation" that were found in the room where the death occurred. It was contended that the alleged suicide note and journal could have been written by either brother. Handwriting exemplars were obtained from the twin brothers' parents. The samples were letters to family members written by the brothers while they were in custody at juvenile detention. From a forensic perspective, many of the individual characteristics could not be relied upon because the writing was inconsistent and was shared by both twin brothers. Ultimately, identification of the handwriting was determined by the handedness of the twin brothers because one had left-handed handwriting characteristics (e.g., crossing t-bars from right to left) while the other brother used right-handed characteristics.

This case illustrates the effects that poor handwriting skill can have in forensic casework and how a handwriting examiner needs to approach the poor writing skill of those who have not been trained properly in handwriting differently from the writing of one who exhibits experience and skill in handwriting, or what is referred to as graphic maturity. Poor handwriting skill among the youth is an ever-growing trend as schools are cutting back on handwriting training due to funding problems, large classroom sizes, and competing curriculum needs. Keyboarding is replacing handwriting training, and in its wake, a generation of individuals with the inability to write cursive or even print properly has been produced. Even older adults who learned cursive when they were young are frequently commenting that they mostly type now and rarely pick up the pen to write anymore. As a result, their handwriting has deteriorated too. Signatures are becoming increasingly illegible, sinuous strokes quickly written with little care or effort.

Articles about the decline in handwriting have been published in the past few years with ominous titles like "The Death of Handwriting" (New York Times, 2009). BBC News discussed "The Slow Death of Handwriting" (2009) while Time Magazine printed "Mourning the Death of Handwriting" which succinctly characterized today's handwriting: "People born after 1980 tend to have a distinctive style of handwriting: a little bit sloppy, a little bit childish and almost never in cursive" (Suddath, 2009). These articles report the fact that our society and a younger generation are writing less, computing more, and texting even more. As a result, there seems little need to teach handwriting to the new generation and even less motivation on the part of youth to learn. This is underscored by the fact that most states in the United States no longer require teaching cursive handwriting in the school curriculum. The Common Core State Standards (CCSS), which most states have adopted, do not require cursive handwriting and only mention handwriting training up to first grade. After first grade, states can choose how to continue handwriting training, or, eliminating handwriting training altogether (Saperstein Associates, 2012). Handwriting training is a concern in other countries like China too where it is predicted that the new generation will not know how to read or write Chinese calligraphy. Published articles are expressing concern that perhaps we are losing an important skill.

Some of the arguments for dropping or limiting handwriting training in school seem logical. For example, handwriting training is laborious and time consuming, and teachers do not have the time needed to train students how to write properly. Additionally, we now live in a digital world and it is more important to learn keyboarding skills than to waste time on learning how to write cursive. However, supporters of cursive handwriting make some equally valid points. How will the new generation sign their signature, even on an electronic tablet if they do not know how to write? This problem is already occurring. Filling out application forms, taking notes, and writing an address on an envelope are still everyday practices. Besides the transcription skills of handwriting, many in the new generation do not even know how to read cursive writing.

In many ways, handwriting is not dying. It is more accurate to say that it is transitioning. Widespread teaching and use of skilled cursive handwriting, by the general population, is a relatively recent skill only in practical use by the common person for the past couple of hundred years. For all practical purposes, the general population has really not been using cursive handwriting for all that long a period of time. Letters from earlier time periods are penned by the wealthy, educated classes, but not always by the uneducated classes. The extent of cursive handwriting in a culture is dependent upon the extent of its literacy. Writing styles are as varied as cultures and their languages and handwriting style reflect the culture of the period. There may be a cyclic trend with handwriting as the simple forms in writing we are producing on digital tablets with a stylus nowadays is not too dissimilar from ancient clay tablets that used a stylus to produce simplistic wedge-like strokes in cuneiform.

2.1 THE NEED FOR HANDWRITING INSTRUCTION

Is handwriting instruction important anymore? With the advent of computers and keyboarding over the past two to three decades, many have said that the need for handwriting is not so important anymore as computer keyboarding replaces the need for using pen and paper. However, there is a problem with legibility in handwriting that the computer has not been able to remedy. Illegible or poorly formed handwriting is seen not only in the infamous "doctor" handwriting but also in educated children and adults. Additionally, there may be reasons besides legibility for children to continue to receive proper training in handwriting. The motor skills needed for handwriting contribute to learning in other areas as well, and multisensory handwriting instruction may provide a tool for helping children with learning disabilities. Tucha and Lange (2005) cite research stating that "children who have difficulty producing legible handwriting often experience frustration, lowered self-esteem, and a decreased level of motivation" (p. 323).

Although computers seem to be a primary cause of neglected handwriting instruction in schools, computers paradoxically could turn out to be one of the reasons why handwriting training may survive in the future. With the increasing use of graphics tablets and digital pens that record text, there could be a trend to replace pen and paper with digital devices thereby preserving a need to produce legible handwriting or handprinting that can be effectively recognized by a computer in order to convert or translate it into text. Computerized handwriting recognition systems may be even less able to read illegible handwriting than humans, providing another practical reason why handwriting needs to conform to minimal standards of legibility.

Research has repeatedly shown that handwriting is an important developmental skill in early childhood education, yet there seems to be an issue with getting this information out to the teachers instructing children in the classrooms. Jones & Christensen (1999) found that while working with first- and second-grade schoolchildren in a handwriting remediation program "teachers indicate that they believed that all the students in participating classes actually received more specific instruction in handwriting than would normally occur, as the teachers became more aware of the processes necessary to develop writing skills" (p. 47). It could be that there is less actual resistance to handwriting instruction than there is a lack of information and training on effective handwriting instruction. According to Graham & Harris (2005), "the No Child Left Behind Act (NCLB) places little emphasis on writing" (p. 19). This Act could be one of the reasons why there are problems in getting knowledge about handwriting instruction into the school system.

Although there is limited information as to quantity and quality of handwriting instruction practiced in the average classroom, a survey of 169 teachers (grades one to three) conducted by Graham & Harris (2005) gives a glimpse of the situation. The survey found that most teachers thought handwriting instruction in the classroom was important and that "ninety percent of the teachers who responded to the handwriting survey indicated that they taught handwriting, providing an average of 72 minutes of instruction per week" (p. 23). They reported that 18% of the students were having difficulty with handwriting and felt that failure to learn to write properly could lead to negative consequences in the quantity and quality of writing, lower grades, and increased time to complete assignments. However, most teachers reported that they did not like to teach handwriting because they were not trained in handwriting instruction. Two-thirds of the teachers were using a "commercial program to teach handwriting" (p. 23). This survey suggests that while teachers think handwriting is valuable and necessary in education, they seem to lack the resources to effectively teach handwriting.

The commercial programs most widely followed by teachers provide copybooks for children and are based upon a strategy called "Trace & Copy" (Nelson, 2006). While this strategy sells workbooks, it is not so effective for developing the skills needed for fluent, automatic handwriting. The fact that school systems regularly find the need to look for a different program is proof of the consistent failure. The lack of effective teacher training leads to selection of a "different program" based upon the same failed strategy. Teachers on selection committees are not aware of the need to look for alternative programs that include multisensory learning activities which include fluent movement as a goal.

The act of tracing models with a pencil demands visual guidance of the movements. The skilled application of handwriting movement involves the motor system primarily (Bartolomeo et al., 2002; Teulings & Romero, 2003). The fluent movements that result in individuality of the traces are goal-oriented, smooth, and rhythmic. The visual feedback system cannot guide this kind of movement. The lack of effective methods training at the college level leaves the new classroom teacher totally dependent upon these commercial programs because they have not been introduced to the background on motor learning or methods that include the instruction of fluent movement as part of the learning experience.

2.2 THE IMPORTANCE OF HANDWRITING

Although word processing and e-mail have replaced many handwritten tasks, there are still several tasks that require legible handwriting. It is not unusual for prospective employers to disregard applications of employment candidates where the handwriting or handprinting is illegible or sloppy. Litigation can result from poorly scripted and illegible prescriptions written by doctors. In fact, there are handwriting remediation programs specifically designed for doctors. The postal service is plagued with illegibly addressed envelopes. There are many examples of the daily application of handwriting, including making out checks, signing receipts, filling out forms, addressing an envelope, writing a card, taking notes, or writing a list (Ediger, 2002; Stempel-Mathey & Wolf, 1999). Some people have a predisposed attitude about others based upon how one's handwriting looks. It is not uncommon for people to make critical remarks about messy or illegible handwriting. Studies have shown that teachers give lower grades for papers that exhibit handwriting dysfluency (Graham et al., 2000, 2001). Graphics tablets are also increasingly being used, which may result in an ever greater need for legible handwriting in order for the recognition software to "read" the handwriting. From a social and ecological perspective, Bruinsma & Nieuwenhuis (1991) claim that "handwriting is an important skill in cultural and social life...writing has not received the attention it deserves in the school curriculum considering the important role that it plays in children's cultural development" (p. 41).

In the early stages of child learning and development, handwriting provides a direct connection or pathway between the brain and the hand for developing literacy. The complex motor processes needed for handwriting, spelling, and compositional writing requires an integration that reinforces language skills in the developing brain. Research has shown that spelling, reading, and writing are reinforced when handwriting is involved (Edwards, 2003; Graham et al., 2000; Jones & Christensen, 1999; Maeland & Karlsdottir, 1991). According to Berninger & Amtmann (2003) "handwriting is more than just a motor act. Handwriting is 'language by hand'" (p. 346). However, if handwriting is not learned properly, poor handwriting acquisition can have an inhibitory effect on compositional writing (Edwards, 2003).

There are few motor tasks that link the body and the brain so intimately as handwriting. The fine motor skill required for handwriting in combination with short-term and long-term memory and language acquisition has benefits for the developing brain that few other activities can replicate. It has been found that a multisensory or kinesthetic approach to learning benefits both disabled and nonlearning disabled children (Laszlo & Broderick, 1991; Stempel-Mathey & Wolf, 1999). Handwriting is a multisensory activity that helps with fine motor coordination, memory, and cognitive development. Adams (as cited in Stempel-Mathey & Wolf, 1999) states that handwriting "may contribute valuably toward the development of those fine motor skills that determine the willingness as well as the ability to write" (p. 258).

More recently, researchers have found that without proper handwriting instruction, children can have difficulty in reading and writing specifically in tasks such as retrieving letters from memory, reproducing letters on paper, accurate spelling, and extracting meaning from text (Berninger, 2012; Case-Smith, 2012; Peverly, 2012). Neurological studies on how the brain responds to different tasks involving text showed that there was significantly more brain activation when children wrote letters than when they typed or traced letters (James, 2012).

2.3 HANDWRITING INSTRUCTION METHODS

There is a wide variety of handwriting instructional methods available in the marketplace and to teachers in the classroom. This perhaps indicates a trend to allow freedom for the child to express individual preferences in the classroom. Some teachers allow students to choose print or cursive, and there is considerably less attention toward regimenting or standardizing handwriting training. In many cases, this results in less practice and less development in handwriting. Practice is necessary in order for handwriting skills to become automatic so that the handwriting process does not interfere with compositional writing. Research shows that a lack of adequate instruction in handwriting results in poor writing composition. Jones & Christensen (1999) were concerned that a lack of automaticity in handwriting could "result in lower motivation to learn in the future, loss of self-efficacy, development of external locus of control, and avoidance of writing tasks" (p. 48). Because both handwriting and keyboarding are necessary tools for the expression of language and communication, both need to be taught in the curriculum. It is especially important that handwriting is introduced in the early stages of education so that the task becomes more habitual at a young age. It seems a logical process that drawing and handwriting exercises are introduced prior to keyboarding. Handwriting involves a more intensive and concentrated link between body and brain that may even facilitate faster and more fluent keyboarding skills later.

The wide variety of training methods available for handwriting instruction certainly allow for individuality in expression for both the learner and the teacher. While the regimented processes used in the past helped to ingrain the habitual writing movements into the brain and the generation of students instructed in this method still write with a high degree of esthetics and legibility, some of the instruction methods were harsh. For instance, some children were forced to write with their non-dominant hand and were subjected to both verbal and physical abuse. These types of practices are no longer acceptable, but the current attitude may be too lax. Continual training in handwriting exercises is imperative in order for handwriting to become a habitual skill. Further, handwriting provides an excellent opportunity for educators to infuse multisensory exercises into the curriculum, which have been shown to benefit all types of learners including the learning disabled (Birsh, 1999).

The National Research Council has established specific goals for writing in kindergarten (Edwards, 2003). Some of these goals included the ability to write one's own name and the names of friends, writing in upper and lowercase, and some writing of letters and words. A comparison of handwriting instruction methods showed that the use of cue cards that diagram letter production and writing from memory produced better results than other traditional methods (such as repeated copying and imitating letters) (Berninger & Amtmann, 2003; Berninger, et al., 1997; Edwards, 2003). These studies employed a series of handwriting instructional approaches that utilize motor imitation, visual cues, memory retrieval, visual cues plus memory retrieval, copy, and control (Edwards, 2003, p. 142). In a study by Jones & Christensen (1999), remediation in the handwriting of first-grade children was found to improve both their handwriting and compositional fluency. In the Graham et al. (2000) study, first-grade subjects exhibiting slow handwriting and poor writing skills and control subjects were provided with training in addition to that which they were receiving in the classroom. The model-based training maintained that "writing a letter requires retrieving and holding the letter in working memory, accessing the corresponding motor program, setting the parameters for the program (e.g., establishing the size of the letter and speed of the writing), and executing it" (p. 621). The results of the study found that both groups (disabled and nondisabled control subjects) benefited from the handwriting instruction and showed an increase in both handwriting and compositional fluency. The researchers warn against neglecting the development of handwriting skills and state that "if educators want to improve the writing of these students, they need to focus not just on the content and process of writing, but on transcription skills such as handwriting as well" and add that "explicit supplemental instruction that helps young children write letters accurately and quickly can increase the probability that they will become skilled writers" (p. 631). The remedial handwriting instruction provided to first and second graders in the Jones & Christensen (1999) study was not "resource consuming" and its benefits outweighed the negligible cost (p. 48). The handwriting instruction was comprised of modeling letters, cues for proper letter construction, multisensory activities that included colors, memory-building skills, air writing activities, and the student recording his/her improvements.

A device that can be used to engage the attention of early writers is teaching students how to write their name. Haney (2002) cites several studies where children identify with their names and prefer the letters in their name to other letters in the alphabet. Haney discusses how name writing places handwriting within a meaningful context for the young writer. Possible exercises involving name writing are also provided by Haney including signing in and name-of-the-week activities and brainstorming words beginning with the letters of the student's name.

Stempel-Mathey & Wolf (1999) recommend the use of "all four sensory pathways: visual, auditory, kinesthetic, and tactile" in handwriting training (p. 264). The authors provide detail into the principles of multisensory teaching including good posture, proper pencil grasp, writing implement, paper, paper position, and motivation. Students were more motivated when they actively participated in identifying what needed remediation in their handwriting. The student is taught to verbally repeat letters as they are written and is encouraged to do activities such as air writing. The printed and cursive alphabet letters were taught in similar groups rather than by letter. This practice corresponds with the recommendations in a study by Graham et al. (2001) where it was found that certain letters were more difficult to execute for young writers and created problems with illegibility.

2.4 INFLUENCE OF LEARNING DISABILITIES ON HANDWRITING

Research using digital handwriting technology has given us new information about learning disabilities and how they manifest in handwriting. For the handwriting examiner, knowledge about literacy level and how learning disabilities may manifest in handwriting can be important when evaluating the writing for individuality and range of variation. The case study involving the 14-year-old twin mentioned at the beginning of the chapter illustrates how graphic maturity and learning disabilities can potentially affect the handwriting in a way that complicates the analysis. There is a need for the handwriting examiner to exhibit caution in forming opinions on such cases. Not only is there the issue of graphic maturity but also the increased variability caused by learning disabilities and their related medications. Any identifying characteristics found in the writing would need to be carefully evaluated as they may be highly fluctuating throughout the script and, as a result, potentially unreliable.

A recent study found that learning disabilities are increasing among those aged 3–17 years and are more prevalent among males and children who come from low-income households (Centers for Disease Control and Prevention, 2011). This data also suggests that those with learning disabilities may be more inclined toward committing crimes or be associated with crimes. Other studies have found a connection between learning disabilities and self-destructive behavior. Poor handwriting skill has been associated with depression, suicide, and learning disabilities. McBride & Siegel (1997) opined that neurological dysfunction may be the root cause for learning disabilities that in turn lead to depression and suicide in adolescents. Learning disability is determined from the handwriting by evaluating spelling, grammar, syntax, and handwriting skill. It was found that there were significant deficiencies in these areas in the handwriting of adolescent suicides in comparison to healthy controls. In evaluating the handwriting, blind subjects were used to rate handwriting errors that included "incorrectly formed letters, confusions…, and scratch-outs" (p. 656). From a juvenile justice perspective, it is expected that suicide notes, anonymous or threatening letters to schools, and graffiti are more likely produced by those with poor handwriting skill and learning disabilities (Fig. 2.2).

Studies on the writing conventions of those with learning disabilities found that problems occurred in the following way: "illegible writing, letters are frequently in reverse order, there are many mistakes in the writing of words as well as mistakes in the use of punctuation and mistakes in the use of capital letters" (Akcin, 2012).

Learning disabilities that only affect handwriting are referred to as dysgraphia. Dysgraphia is a far-reaching condition, though, and can be acquired when certain conditions, such as Alzheimer's, are present. While it relates primarily to the transcription skills needed to produce handwriting, it can affect other fine motor skills as well. Some of the handwriting features associated with dysgraphia include spelling, wrong words, writing fatigue, problems forming certain letters, illegibility, inconsistent size, and mixing capitals with lower-case letters. The stress caused by writers with dysgraphia can lead to impatience

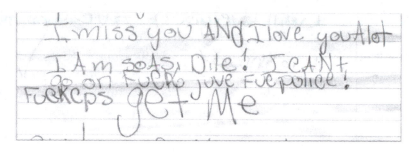

Fig. 2.2 Example of adolescent writing about suicide: "I am so AsiDile!" The handwriting shows signs of dysgraphia (e.g., mixing capitals with lower-case letters, inconsistent size, and misspelling).

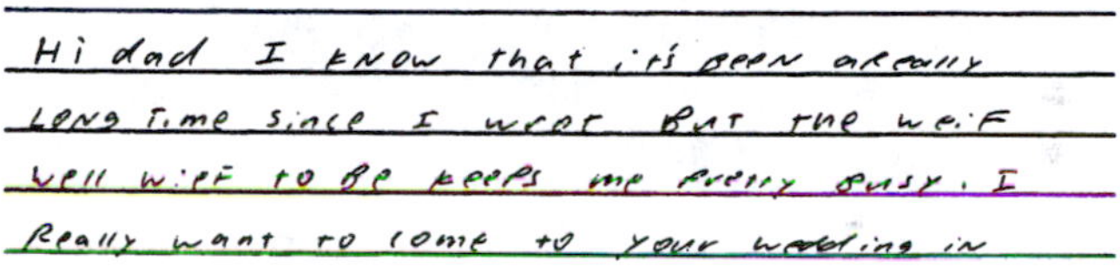

Fig. 2.3 Example of dyslexic writing with transposed letters in the word "wife" twice (lines 2 and 3).

and frustration with the writing act, which further leads to careless and poorly formed script. Other types of learning disabilities can affect handwriting as well as other learning functions. For example, dyslexia is associated with letter or numeral reversals in handwritten script and transposed letters in spelling (Fig. 2.3).

Children diagnosed with attention deficit hyperactivity disorder (ADHD) may have "underlying motor impairment" (Langmaid et al., 2012). Using kinematic research methods and digital tablet technology, ADHD subjects wrote handwriting-related tasks. In comparison to healthy controls, the ADHD subjects showed inconsistency in handwriting size and the severity of the ADHD predicted poorer handwriting.

2.5 FORENSIC PROBLEMS WITH ILLEGIBLE AND PRINTED HANDWRITING

It is an accepted principle in handwriting identification that one cannot successfully imitate the fluent handwriting skill of another if the former does not possess the latter's level of handwriting skill (Huber & Headrick, 1999). In other words, if a person can only print instead of write in cursive, that person will not be able to imitate a fluent, complex, and highly skilled cursive signature. However, the person with handwriting skill can imitate the writing of someone with poor handwriting skill. Sometimes in such cases, however, the forger's own level of skill is too fluent for the forgery which in turn does not match the unskilled genuine writing samples that are used for comparison.

A problem that has developed with signatures over the past few decades involves not only illegibility but also the complexity of the signature. It is universally accepted that if a person signs their name with the "X" symbol, this is an indication that the person is illiterate and cannot sign their name. More recently, though, people are tending to sign their names ever increasingly with very simple loops, dashes, or illegible threaded scrawls which provide about as much identifying information as signing one's name with an "X".

While doctors' writings are frequently commented upon for their illegibility and overly simplified style, many people are writing this way, especially in their signatures. It is not uncommon for some writers to have more than one signature style; a complex, more carefully written signature on a formal document and another, informal signature used for signing credit card receipts or less important documents, usually written while the signer is in a hurry. Sometimes, signers have a few signature styles all dependent on their personal idiosyncrasies that can also be dependent on the circumstances in which they are writing their signature. This is one of the reasons why document examiners request several examples of a person's signature so that they can determine what is referred to as "range of variation." The range of variation can be different from person to person; some signers have consistent signatures while others can have signatures that are erratic and changeable. Additionally, it is not uncommon for people to change their signature, even slightly, over a period of time which is the reason why document examiners need to compare questioned signatures against contemporaneously written comparison signatures.

But the issue of oversimplified signatures consisting of simple loops or thready scrawls has been addressed in research studies that show that forensic handwriting examiners provide more correct opinions when evaluating highly complex signatures than when evaluating signatures with low complexity (Sita et al., 2002). The research based on what is known as complexity theory also developed a mathematical formula that could quantitatively rate the complexity level of a signature based on the number of its intersection points and turning points (Found & Rogers, 1998). The theory provides a three-level rating scale that allows the examiner to more definitively assess whether a signature has enough complexity to provide an opinion. For example, if a signature is comprised of a single loop with three turning points and one intersection, according to the theory and when calculating the formula, the complexity rating for this type of signature is so low that it is advised that the document examiner offer an inconclusive opinion on the signature. This signifies that the examiner does not have enough evidence in which to form an opinion. A middle level is also calculated that allows document examiners to offer qualified opinions while a highly complex signature would allow for unqualified opinions or opinions of certainty. While the trend toward careless signature styles may not have been the motivating reason behind the handwriting complexity research, the need for such research was certainly timely as it coincided with a trend in deteriorating signatures (Fig. 2.4).

Part of the reason why a person uses a signature is to establish a unique and identifying mark. Writing with an overly simplified signature is not only illegible (most of the time) but is also not a very secure way in which to establish or protect identity. Even a person with no handwriting skill is capable of successfully imitating a simple mark. The reason why document examiners offer inconclusive opinions on such signatures is due to the ease in which such signatures can be imitated. The combination of a simple signature with a high range of variation makes signature identification even more problematic as it helps to disguise the forger's own variation from the model which they are copying.

A signature does not need to be written in cursive in order to be legally valid. Printed signatures and the "X" mark are also accepted as signatures. The problem with printed signatures is similar to the problem with overly simplified signatures. Printing tends to be easier

Fig. 2.4 Complex signature (left) versus a simple, noncomplex signature (right).

to imitate than cursive writing because it requires less skill. Cursive writing, with its connections, produces fluent, smooth curves that are frequently difficult to imitate. Printing, with its isolated structures, is easier to simulate since the writer does not have to imitate the fluency of the connected curves and can break between printed elements. However, not all printing styles lack fluency. Many people who consider themselves "printers" use a combination of cursive and print which also has fluently written, connected forms.

2.6 SUMMARY

The decline in handwriting training has forensic implications since handwriting identification is partially based on class characteristics from penmanship models, and handwriting fluency is partially relied upon in differentiating between natural and forged handwriting. Despite the fact that handwriting instruction time in classrooms has been reduced, and cursive has been eliminated in some instances, research has established the importance of handwriting instruction in reading, writing, spelling, and composition in school-age children. Fluent, practiced, and overlearned handwriting skill is associated with better academic performance. Researchers have also developed handwriting instruction methods that help develop fluency in handwriting. In handwriting identification cases that involve poor handwriting skill or learning disorders, these conditions create problems with handwriting variability and complexity. In forensic handwriting examination, if the signature is too simple, there is not enough handwritten material for the handwriting examiner to form an opinion about authorship. A complexity model has been developed to help handwriting examiners express a meaningful level of opinion on signatures with too little complexity.

CHAPTER 3

Advances in Handwriting Research and Technology

Many of the problematic areas affecting handwriting identification have been challenged over the past few decades using advanced techniques in digital technology and electronic handwriting capturing devices and software. Handwriting identification research has benefited by the extensive medical research into handwriting movement disorders which has enabled handwriting experts to not only validate many of their methods and observations but also find quantitative methods for dynamic movement. Handwriting identification is no longer just about the way letters are formed; it is also about the fluency and rapidity in which letters are formed. Forensic handwriting examiners used to make estimates about speed, but now they have the tools to quantify speed and to validate the features of a fast or slow handwriting movement.

The result of medical research into the effects of motor disorders, such as Parkinson's disease (PD), and the patient's medication cycles has become an integral part of forensic handwriting identification research. Understanding how handwriting is affected by movement disorders and by medication use is especially important now that these issues are more frequently arising in handwriting examination casework.

The following case study illustrates the importance of knowing the research on how medical conditions influence handwriting. Mary is an elderly woman with PD. As the disease progresses, she also exhibits symptoms of dementia. Because of her mental state, Mary is provided with a caretaker who helps her with her daily needs. The caretaker has access to Mary's checkbook and other financial instruments. Although the caretaker is not a signer on Mary's checking account, she does fill out checks for Mary, including the dollar amounts. Some of these checks are made out to the caretaker. Surprisingly, the checks to the caretaker appear for large dollar amounts, exceeding the usual wages of a caretaker. However, the signatures on these checks are not questioned for they resemble Mary's signature which is known to show signs of decline (e.g., tremor, poor alignment, and even misspelling of her name). The characteristics are typical of those found in PD patients. After Mary's death, an insurance instrument is presented by the caretaker, naming the caretaker as the sole beneficiary. This document is disputed by Mary's relatives who claim she would not have signed the insurance instrument. The claimants suspected fraud by the caretaker. The caretaker had been transferring Mary's assets into her own name, and had continued to do so after Mary's death. The signature's overall style resembled Mary's known signature samples, except for a few critical features. The first critical feature appeared when comparing the signature with other signatures that Mary had written at about the same time. The questioned signature featured blunt endings and beginnings. In addition, it showed a few other simulation characteristics. However, the most critical oversight on the part of the forger involved timing. The forger had used an earlier model of Mary's signature, prior to the onset of her dementia, to guide her own forgery efforts. The date of the document and its associated signature did not match the extent of deterioration of Mary's true signature at that point in time. When the signatures were laid out sequentially in demonstration at trial, the questioned signature clearly stood out from the known signatures (Fig. 3.1).

A kinematical analysis of handwriting offers opportunities for research into information about the static trace analyzed by document examiners. While information from the static trace may be limited, knowledge of the kinematics of handwriting gives the opportunity for handwriting experts to understand what can be analyzed and evaluated in the static trace. It also provides new avenues for research. Extensive research exists in the medical literature on the kinematical handwriting analysis of motor disorders. Although limited, some research has also been performed on the kinematical handwriting features in normal

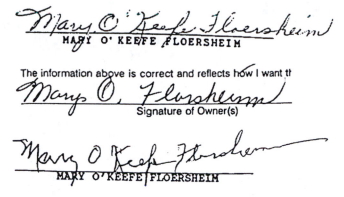

Fig. 3.1 Known and questioned samples of Mary's signature. First signature is written before she was diagnosed with PD and dementia. Middle signature is a disputed, questioned signature. Third signature is written while Mary has dementia. The disputed signature was dated during the time Mary had dementia.

handwriting, disguised writing, and simulation of another person's handwriting. Effects of psychiatric disorders and the effects of their respective medications, and the effects of alcohol on handwriting have been examined kinematically, using electronic handwriting devices and associated software. Motor control researchers using digital tablets and handwriting measurement software have found evidence that suggests that writers show different velocity profiles when simulating than when using their normal handwriting.

The capture of electronic signatures (discussed in Chapters 4 and 5) would not have been possible without the strides in handwriting recording technology that have been accomplished over the past three decades. However, methods of extracting dynamic handwriting measures are not new. Freeman (1918) and Saudek (1978) performed experiments in child and adult handwriting using motion-picture photos and cinematographic exposures taken at speeds of 1/25 of a second (also known as the Freeman Unit) to obtain information about the speed of writing. Extracting dynamic information from the static trace, through location of interaction points on the writing trace produced by movements of muscle-joint systems, was proposed by Hardy (1992). Although information from the static trace may be somewhat limited, dynamic information on factors such as speed, velocity, and other characteristics can be observed from the static trace and correlated with the characteristics of forgery reported in the document examination literature (Hilton, 1993; Huber & Headrick, 1999; Leung et al., 1993a, 1993b).

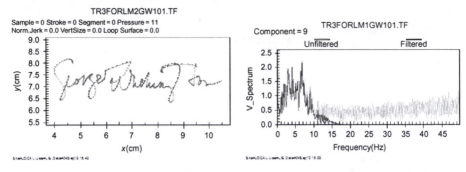

Fig. 3.2 Handwriting sample (left) and its frequency spectrum data captured using NeuroScript MovAlyzeR software.

The next major step forward in understanding the physics of handwriting involved the invention or introduction of computerized handwriting movement recordings. Computerized systems allow movement and position to be recorded at a high and constant rate. The rate is expressed in hertz (Hz), which is a unit of frequency based on the number of cycles per second of a periodic phenomenon. The hertz unit is named after Heinrich Rudolf Hertz, who explored electromagnetic waves. Software systems record the material at a specific rate in hertz. This approach to recording movement is possible because handwriting is a cyclic, time-based movement showing peaks at specific frequencies. The handwriting recording can therefore be described completely in frequency waves. This allows for scientific study and measurement based on the dynamic movement of the handwriting in addition to the static, form-based trace written on paper (Fig. 3.2).

3.1 HANDWRITING AND MOVEMENT DISORDERS

There has been considerable experimental research on the effects of motor disorders on handwriting and on graphic exercises such as spirals and repetitive letter patterns. Many studies also examine the effects that physical therapy and pharmacological treatments may have on motor movements. Much of what we know about the handwriting movement profile of motor disorders is based on handwriting samples captured using electronic technology. Studies on the problems associated with movement disorders such as PD and essential tremor (ET) offer clues toward their handwriting characterization. This will help in differentiating true health effects from simulation of these health effects in forgery both in the static trace and the online analysis. Studying the problems that can occur when handwriting is affected by health

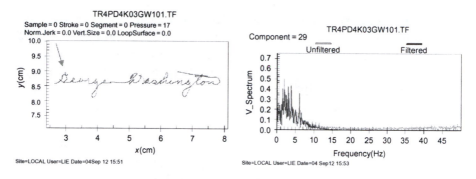

Fig. 3.3 Example of Parkinson's handwriting tremor and its frequency spectrum data.

conditions is important as it is considered a potentially limiting factor when assessing simulation in handwriting samples, especially since simulation and handwriting affected by health factors can share some of the same handwriting characteristics such as tremor, dysfluency, and hesitations. Many of the studies reviewed in this section were previously summarized by Harralson (2005).

There are a number of motor disorder conditions where handwriting is affected by the severity of the condition and coexisting disorders. PD is one of the more prevalent and extensively researched motor disorder problems. The movement symptoms of PD influence the fine motor movement necessary to produce smooth and fluent handwriting. Tremor creates a ragged, shaky line quality; rigidity causes jerky and angular movements; and bradykinesia produces slow handwriting movement, which can lead to small and uncoordinated handwriting or micrographia (Hristova & Koller, 2000; Pal et al., 2002; Phillips et al., 1991; Teulings et al., 2002). PD patients, especially as the disease progresses, tend to avoid handwriting tasks because it is stressful and difficult (Phillips et al., 1991).

Kinematic handwriting research corroborates the primary symptoms that form the diagnosis of PD movement disorders. Research describes PD handwriting (in comparison to healthy handwriting) as having variable acceleration peaks, stroke sizes, or micrographia (small handwriting size) (Teulings et al., 2002, p. 315). Boisseau (as cited in Teulings et al., 1997) observed that "PD handwriting can be characterized by various types of dysfluencies: lack of control, abrupt changes in direction, tremor, slowness, hesitation, rigidity, variability of baseline, and in some cases, micrographia" (p. 159) (Fig. 3.3).

Parkinsonian tremor is a resting tremor, which stops during programmed movements. As the disease progresses slowness is observed causing more irregular movements and sometimes action tremor is present which results in a frequency peak in a handwriting recording. Pal et al. (2002) note that "approximately 70% of patients notice tremor as the first symptom" and it is characterized as having a 3–5 Hz (frequency) with rhythmic "pill-rolling" movements and varying amplitude (p. 43). Symptoms typically start on one side of the body and with progression of the disease, both sides are affected. Additionally, the dominant hand (or side of the body) is typically the side affected with more severity (Uitti et al., 2005).

Rigidity, another common PD symptom, is typically present in the wrists and is described as "an increased resistance to passive movement" (Pal et al., 2002). PD patients demonstrate not only rigidity and akinesia, but also "freezing of movement" (Dietz as cited in Joseph, 1996, p. 337). This resistance or frozen movement can cause angular and/or awkward handwriting where rounded movements should be present in smoothly curved letter formations. Hesitation might also occur in the handwriting line quality where fluent, unbroken movement is expected.

Bradykinesia is defined as slowness of movement with slowness increasing as PD advances. Pal et al. (2002) claim that "bradykinesia is the most disabling component" of PD, and that "bradykinesia and rigidity usually occur together and in most cases are comparable in severity" (p. 44). This indicates that slow movement may characterize PD handwriting.

Other features that can characterize PD include micrographia and variance in the control of movement size and speed. Not only do instances of micrographia appear in about 10–15% of PD cases but patients typically "are unable to sustain normal-sized writing for more than a few letters" (McLennan as cited in Phillips et al., 1991, p. 302). Van Gemmert et al. (2003) indicate that "control of movement amplitude and speed may be the source of two distinctive symptoms often observed in such patients, namely hypometric and bradykinetic movements" (p. 1502). It is further noted that movements of increased complexity are problematic for PD patients and can be seen in corresponding complex handwriting movements: "if it is assumed that an alternating letter pattern—for example, *i*'s (sharp reversals) and *l*'s (curved reversals)—is more complex than a letter pattern of *l*'s only, patients with PD should be more affected than age matched controls by the alternating letter pattern, which requires the subject to make alternations between sharp and curved reversals" (pp. 1502–1503). It was found that PD patients had a harder time writing the more complex movements when required to increase size and speed. Similar results were found by Longstaff et al. (2003) in a study of PD patients with micrographia and age-matched controls. The PD patients demonstrated more movement variability when increasing size and speed in a spiral writing task. It was hypothesized that PD patients choose to write smaller in order to control movement variability.

Some researchers have shown that PD patients exhibiting micrographia can consciously alter their handwriting. It was found that external cues increased the size and speed of the handwriting or drawing in PD patients (Longstaff et al., 2003; Oliveira et al., 1997; Van Gemmert et al., 1999a). This suggests that if a PD patient directs attention to the handwriting task, changes in the size and speed of the handwriting can be made. Further, writing guidelines enable the patient to write at normal sizes as suggested by the guidelines.

Essential tremor (ET) is another common movement disorder that can impact handwriting. It has some features common to PD and the two disorders can coexist. Tremor is the primary clinical feature of ET and manifests as a high-amplitude action tremor. ET mainly affects the upper extremities, but it particularly affects the hands (Biary & Koller, 1987). Aside from pharmacological treatments, ET can fluctuate due to stress and day-to-day variance. Additionally, tremor may not appear consistently throughout the handwriting pattern.

Many ET patients are socially embarrassed by the tremor that occurs in the hands and in the shaking of the head. While interviewing patients, Koller et al. (1986) found that "writing a signature was a common problem, particularly in public, and most patients had discontinued all activities that involved writing" (p. 1002).

In many handwriting identification cases, acquiring exemplars from the subject writer demonstrating the effects of a motor disorder is not possible because the writer is either incapacitated (due to the effects of the disorder) or deceased. Accurate assessment of movement disorders from handwriting is frequently dependent on an adequate number of exemplars demonstrating the writer's day-to-day variation, possible deterioration, and/or medical treatment. This is complicated by patients who, because their handwriting lacks fluency, are not particularly inclined to write because it is too difficult or they are embarrassed.

Medical research offers information about motor system individualization and disorder as these are manifested in the static handwriting trace. The research indicates that differential analysis between PD and ET based on qualitative observations of handwriting is possible in some cases. PD can exhibit micrographia, abrupt changes in direction, lack of control, slowness, hesitation, rigidity (causing angular and awkward formations), variability of baseline, variance in control of movement size and speed, and tremor (especially as the disease progresses). While ET exhibits tremor during an action writing task, it may not be present throughout the handwriting pattern. The characterization of motor disorders can aid in handwriting identification cases when the handwriting exhibits dysfluency.

3.2 HANDWRITING AND PSYCHIATRIC DISORDERS

Recent clinical research has made significant contributions to understanding the causes and the effects of handwriting production exhibiting dysfunction. Some research includes the quantification of handwriting impairment in neurological conditions such as PD. In neuropsychiatric conditions, clinical handwriting research has been able to make comparisons of healthy control subjects with patients who have obsessive-compulsive disorder (OCD), schizophrenia, depression, and posttraumatic stress disorder (PTSD). The research has shown that handwriting impairment patterns in various neuropsychiatric conditions can help the clinician in diagnosing symptoms or assessing severity. Many of the studies also examine the handwriting effects of psychiatric medications for assessment purposes. For the handwriting expert, understanding clinical research assessments can aid the handwriting identification expert in explaining unusual or extraordinary handwriting production, especially if the handwriting is showing signs of change due to psychiatric episodes or use of medications.

The intimate connection between hand and brain indicates that neurological and neuropsychiatric disorders affect the motor movements associated with handwriting production. There are numerous, interconnected processes involved in the human production of handwriting. The brain controls the motor system and visual perception in the production of highly complex and coordinated movements that send nerve impulses through the central nervous system to guide the arm, the wrist, the hand, and the fingers in producing what Hermann et al. (2002) call "overlearned" handwriting movements (p. 1086). The brain, which is the controlling mechanism in handwriting production, is influenced by factors such as language processing, memory and learning of handwriting forms, the perception of and individual interpretation of handwriting forms, and experience and skill in production of these forms.

With so many neurological and biomechanical processes requiring precise coordination, handwriting production is a remarkable skill. It is not surprising that even minor dysfunction in any of these complex processes can be reflected in fine motor skills, leaving behind the residual effects of the dysfunction in the handwriting trace through uncoordinated movements, pressure and speed irregularities, and tremor. Neurological disorders and brain damage can especially impair handwriting production. Damage to the memory and/or language centers of the brain can create problems in the handwriting images formed in the brain, while degenerative diseases of the nervous system can result in uncoordinated or tremulous handwriting forms.

The complexity of the brain, nervous system, and the motor program involved in the handwriting act can create highly unique and individualized forms that can result in a quantifiably identifiable motor pattern. These complex systems are sensitive to dysfunctions which manifest in the motor system and are detectable in the handwriting trace, creating another identifiable characteristic that is used as a diagnostic tool in the medical profession, but can also be used in handwriting identification.

Tremor is regarded as one of the soft signs in neurological assessment and is found in several degenerative conditions such as PD, Huntington's disease, and multiple sclerosis. In terms of handwriting characterization, there is some crossover between neurological motor disorders and neuropsychiatric disorders. For example, PD and Alzheimer's disease, especially in a highly degenerative state, can include behavioral problems such as dementia. However, there are many Parkinson's patients that do not exhibit behavioral or neuropsychiatric disorders.

Depression has a neurological basis and is one condition in which there has been kinematical research. Depression is defined as feelings of apathy, self-neglect, and a lack of interest. Not surprisingly, clinical handwriting research has found that psychomotor retardation is associated with depression (Mergl et al., 2004a; Tucha et al., 2002), and it is theorized that basal ganglia/thalamo-cortical dysfunction could be a cause for depression. It was found that depressed patients write with less regular velocity than healthy controls. Tucha et al., (2002) measured velocity and stroke acceleration, and found that depressive patients who were taking tricyclic antidepressants (TCAs) also had slower writing time than the healthy control group and depressive patients who were administered selective serotonin reuptake inhibitors (SSRIs). Additionally, the TCA group displayed "a severe dysfluency of handwriting and lower maximum velocities and acceleration of descending strokes than the other groups" (p. 214). It was found that TCAs are not effective in treating psychomotor retardation typical of depression while SSRIs do affect and increase writing speed. In addressing the effect of medications on depression, the researchers pointed out that there have been few studies on the effect of medications on psychomotor skills associated with depression and also noted that TCAs may have the effect of slowing down motor skills while SSRIs may speed up motor skills.

OCD (obsessive-compulsive disorder) is a neurological condition that causes uncontrollable thinking and ritualistic behavior. Like other neurological disorders, OCD has varying degrees of severity and the medications prescribed for this condition can affect the motor control system. Basal ganglia dysfunction has been associated with OCD (Mavrogiorgou et al., 2001). The basal ganglia and the cerebellum provide information to the thalamus for directing finely tuned movements (de Kerckhove & Lumsden, 1988, p. 253). Dysfunction in fine motor movements is considered a neurological "soft" sign in determining OCD, and handwriting factors such as slow writing speed and decreased writing variability were associated with the handwriting of OCD patients in comparison to control subjects. Psychopharmacological treatments tended to normalize these writing factors (Mergl et al., 2004b). According to Mavrogiorgou et al. (2001), micrographia is also associated with OCD, and "repetitive motor pattern performance was not impaired, but rather tended to be even better in patients with OCD than in controls" (p. 605). These results may not be surprising, as the behavioral pattern of OCD patients tends toward careful, controlled movements. Mavrogiorgou et al. confirm this hypothesis: "due to basal ganglia dysfunction, strongly overlearned primitive behaviour patterns can be elicited faster in patients with OCD than in controls; patients with OCD adopt a qualitatively and kinematically different style of handwriting, because they are simply unable to confirm that they are performing the task adequately. This might more accurately reflect their psychopathology (for example, doubt, checking) than any fundamental difficulty in hand motor control" (p. 610–611).

Dementia and delirium are closely linked and can coexist, but Feinberg and Farah (1997) distinctly point out the differences in the two disorders as defined in Diagnostic and Statistical Manual of Mental Disorders (DSM-IV). The definition of delirium is a "disturbance in consciousness, attentional deficits, brief duration of symptoms, and fluctuation in symptoms over time" (p. 500). Dementia is defined as "(1) an impairment in social and occupational functioning and (2) memory and other cognitive deficits" (p. 500). Movement disorders associated with delirium include tremor, abnormal movements, and bizarre posturing (Ibid.). Conditions such as Alzheimer's disease are commonly associated with dementia.

In a study that tested patients with terminal delirium, it was found that handwriting was the most impaired of the language tests administered (Macleod & Whitehead, 1997) and that all patients "made obvious dysgraphic errors" (p. 129). Another important handwriting factor found in this study was the reduplication of letters. It was recommended by the researchers that handwriting samples can be an accurate clinical test for measuring delirium in patients.

Other studies using digital tablets found significant impairment in those with Alzheimer's disease and mild cognitive impairment. Specifically, it was found that the Alzheimer's subjects and those with cognitive impairment "demonstrated slower, less smooth, less coordinated, and less consistent handwriting movements than their healthy counterparts" (Yan et al., 2008, p. 1203). Another study, using a digital tablet for handwriting data collection of Alzheimer's patients diagnosed with dementia, found that the subjects exhibited increased variability in comparison to healthy subjects. This included variability in speed, velocity, and stroke length (Schröter et al., 2003; Slavin et al., 1999). The subjects also increased in perseveration (repetition of units or letter segments). These results were consistently shown whether the patients were taking medication or not. Another comparison of Alzheimer's patients with healthy controls showed that the patients showed an increase in temporal features while the pen pressure was lower (Werner et al., 2006).

Neurological research into the forensic application of cognitive status based on distorted handwriting showed that handwriting variables such as spatial problems and spelling errors could be correlated with neuropsychological scales associated with dementia (Balestrino et al., 2012). This type of handwriting examination would be useful in forensic cases where the person who signed the document in question is now deceased, such as in probate matters where the decedent's Will is in question (Fig. 3.4).

Schizophrenia can take on various forms but is generally related to a split from reality and its symptoms include "disorganized thinking, disturbed perceptions, and inappropriate emotions and actions" (Myers, 2001, p. 580). Schizophrenia is an often mislabeled and overused term. Part of the confusion associated with schizophrenia is the variety of forms in which it can manifest. In some forms of schizophrenia, the motor program is affected. Joseph & Young (1992) state that some of the neurological soft signs associated with movement disorders in schizophrenia include lack of coordination, motor impersistence, poor balance, posturing with stress maneuvers, asymmetric reflexes, astereognosis (inability to determine the form of an object by touch), and agraphesthesia (disorientation of skin sensation across its space).

However, research into how schizophrenia affects handwriting indicates that disorders are caused by more than dysfunction in the motor program. Coron et al. (2000) studied patients diagnosed with paranoid schizophrenia and noted language disorders from the writing samples.

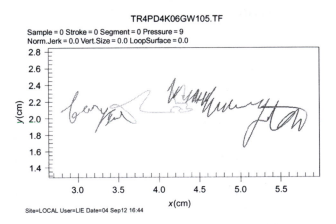

Fig. 3.4 Handwriting sample of a person diagnosed with dementia.

Specifically, it was found that language or writing problems such as graphemic paragraphia were evident (Fig. 3.5).

Antipsychotic medications typically prescribed for schizophrenia can cause a variety of movement disorders including tardive dyskinesia, akathisia, dystonia, Parkinsonism, tremor, bradykinesia, postural abnormalities, muscle rigidity, reduction in size of handwriting, and rhythmic disturbances in handwriting (Gervin & Barnes, 2000).

Kinematic research into how medications affect schizophrenics showed that handwriting can be used as a clinical monitor for medication side effects and is a more reliable measure than observer-based ratings (Caligiuri et al., 2010). Capturing handwriting samples with a digital pen and digital tablet and handwriting movement software, several handwriting features were measured including duration, velocity, acceleration, and smoothness. Comparing the psychiatric patients to healthy controls, it was found that the patients exhibited slower and less fluent writing than controls. Handwriting differences were also observed in response to varying doses of psychotic medications on different days when evaluating patient handwriting. The findings support using handwriting movement as a quantitative measure to evaluate patient response to antipsychotic medication.

Stress or extreme emotional states related to or causing stress can influence handwriting movement. Longstaff & Heath (2003) noted that writers with tremor or motor system degradation had a harder time adapting to writing conditions where mild stress was introduced through the presence of a "loud, annoying sound" (p. 92). However, healthy controls were able to adapt and maintain control by increasing pen pressure, while the tremor group decreased pen pressure.

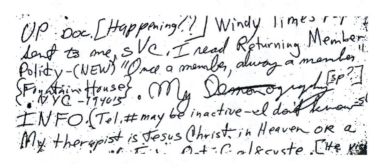

Fig. 3.5 Handwriting sample of a person diagnosed with schizophrenia.

Halder-Sinn et al. (1998) compared samples of accelerated handwriting movements, handwritings performed under mild stress conditions, and control handwritings produced under normal conditions. The researchers did not find noticeable differences between the accelerated handwriting and the stress handwriting groups. However, it was noted that there were some differences between acceleration/stress samples and the control samples: slant of descenders, horizontal extension, exactness of lines, and distance of *i* dots (p. 458).

Loud noises seemed to be the trigger for tremor associated with PTSD in a case study (Walters & Hening, 1992). When the patient was startled, his handwriting became bigger, showed inconsistencies, and exhibited tremor similar to psychogenic tremor. The patient's normal handwriting was moderate in size, exhibiting only a fine kinetic tremor.

Significant progress has been made in the past decade with respect to understanding handwriting production and its associated dysfunctions. The use of the digital writing tablet has helped to quantify components of handwriting production such as speed, fluency, and tremor. The clinical research to date can be used as a standard for future research in areas such as handwriting identification. For example, it was noted in the OCD research that patients had slower handwriting speeds in comparison to control subjects when measured with the digital writing tablet. Research has shown that handwriting experts can make accurate speed comparisons between static trace handwriting samples (Will, 2012). Additionally, experimental research could answer whether handwriting experts can identify the graphic signs associated with OCD and depressive writing and differentiate them from healthy controls. It should be noted, however, that the clinicians who may be using handwriting as a diagnostic tool are usually using the tool in combination with other assessment techniques. Motor control aberrations are usually considered a "soft sign" for diagnosis and it raises questions as to the accuracy of information that can be detected from the static trace alone without the use of the digitizing tablet, other measuring tools, or observations of the patient's symptoms.

As with any clinical assessment, caution is advised in making any diagnosis of a medical or psychiatric nature. The clinical studies can aid the handwriting expert in evaluating unexplainable variations in handwriting as well as give guidance in understanding medical causes for unusual handwriting factors. For the handwriting identification expert, it is important to be aware of organic causes of handwriting variation when examining a collection of standards or questioned writing that is exhibiting factors that are outside of the expected norm or range of variation of the typical writing pattern. It is also useful for the handwriting examiner to have knowledge about the various treatments administered to patients with neurological and neuropsychiatric disorders. Certain treatments can seriously alter the handwriting in such a way that it does not resemble a return to the writer's former pattern (with or without symptoms of the disorder). For example, Tucha et al. (2002) theorized that SSRIs create hyperactivity in depressive patients which could lead to an increase to the writer's motor system (increasing handwriting speed) while TCAs depress or slow down the motor system.

Although the handwriting expert cannot testify or report as to the clinical cause of unusual handwriting manifestations, motor control research is helpful for explaining possible causes so that inaccurate assessments can be avoided. Clinical studies also provide a base for handwriting experts to use in research that addresses concerns such as comparing unusual handwriting forms to simulated writings and forming correct opinions.

3.3 OTHER FACTORS INFLUENCING HANDWRITING

Aside from strictly medical-related applications, handwriting kinematics has also been used to explore some other areas that are known to influence handwriting. The research we know, about how substances such as alcohol and caffeine affect motor system performance, is updated with kinematics research as well as with research into other areas such as sleep deprivation, fatigue, and posture.

There are several studies extant relating to the effects of handwriting and alcohol. Among the more recent studies, one used a digital tablet for handwriting sample capture. In a kinematic analysis of handwriting written under the influence of alcohol, the electronically captured handwriting-related samples showed that alcohol affected stroke length in handwriting samples (Phillips et al., 2009). Alcohol also affected handwriting acceleration and the ballistic movement of the writing was less in the alcohol-induced subjects than in the controls (Fig. 3.6).

In a study on the effects of caffeine on handwriting, it was shown that caffeine improves motor performance. In a kinematic study using a

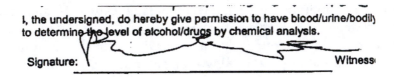

I, the undersigned, do hereby give permission to have blood/urine/bodily
to determine the level of alcohol/drugs by chemical analysis.

Signature: _____   Witness

Fig. 3.6 Alcohol-influenced signature.

digital tablet, subjects were administered caffeine resulting in increased handwriting fluency and an increase in velocity and acceleration in the handwriting exercises (Tucha et al., 2006). Caffeine's effects were shown to not only speed up the handwriting movement, an expected effect, but also improve accuracy through fluency.

Handwriting can be such a sensitive barometer of movement dysfunction that it has even been kinematically demonstrated that sleep deprivation can also affect handwriting movement (Conduit, 2008). Specifically, it was found that after 24 hours of sleep deprivation, the subjects showed a significant difference in the spatial aspects of their handwriting, namely, an increase in the amount of writing space used by the subject in comparison to handwriting samples recorded after the subjects had had a normal night's sleep.

Fatigue influences handwriting, especially in those with motor disorders and this can be induced through extended handwriting tasks. In PD patients, fatigue can increase micrographia, tremor, rigidity, errors, and speed reduction (which may be related to increased rigidity). Fatigue particularly plays a role in persons with neuro-musculoskeletal disorders or disabilities such as PD and ET. The motor control literature has reported that when PD patients are fatigued, they tend to reduce their writing size, thus exhibiting micrographia. It has been shown that micrographia increases with increased processing demands (Van Gemmert et al., 1999b, 2001). Micrographia is sensitive to visual feedback, as it can be increased or decreased by amplified or reduced vertical scaling of the visual feedback, respectively (Teulings et al., 2002).

Among healthy writers, it has been reported that fatigue causes deteriorative effects in handwriting (Lou et al., 2001; Provins & Magliaro, 1989). Research on healthy writers has shown that fatigue more severely affects those with poor writing skill. Fatigue can result in an increase in size, length, lateral spacing, errors, baseline variance, speed, and slope (Poulin, 1999). In evaluating the handwriting research for movement disorder patients and healthy writers, patients exhibit more variance in their handwriting as a result of fatigue than normal controls. This was demonstrated in a kinematic study that compared the handwriting fatigue effects between motor disorder patients and healthy controls (Harralson et al., 2009). In comparing the two groups, controls were faster than the patients in both the nonfatigue and fatigue conditions. However, in comparing the conditions among the individual subjects, some motor-impaired and/or fatigued writers used unorthodox strategies to handle tasks involving repetitive writing that can cause fatigue and subsequent deterioration of their handwriting (i.e., switching from cursive to printing). The study also showed that motor disordered patients exhibit more variability than healthy controls when performing repetitive writing tasks that can cause fatigue.

In forensic handwriting problems, even subtle handwriting changes caused by fatigue can complicate handwriting identification because it relies on a pattern-based observation of a writer's natural range of variation. Before an identification or elimination can be provided, the forensic document examiner needs to rule out certain handwriting conditions (such as fatigue) that may be the cause for increased differences between handwriting samples. Fatigue can occur in commonplace business transactions that require the signing of multiple documents, such as real estate and probate transactions. Handwriting fatigue can also occur during "request handwriting standard" sessions which require persons to sometimes produce a large number of handwriting samples through copying or dictation.

An important study on writing conditions, such as posture and position of the writer in relationship to writing implements, was conducted by Sciacca et al. (2008). The subjects were placed in awkward signing positions while their handwriting was captured kinematically on a digital tablet with a digital pen to determine the level of variability between postural conditions. The positions included a normal condition with the subject writing at a desk as a control and awkward writing conditions such as subjects kneeling on the ground. The results showed that the within-subject variability increased for the awkward or unusual position, but there was only a slight increase relating to the lowercase words. The personal idiosyncrasies were present in the writing samples in all postural conditions, implying that a forensic analysis even in awkward signing conditions is still reliable. This research is important for evaluations involving electronic signature tablets as the postural conditions in electronic signing situations can also be awkward.

3.4 HANDWRITING AND SIMULATION

Using digital tablet technology, there has been research showing the link between observing dynamic movement in handwriting and the impaired or inhibited movement processes associated with forged or simulated handwriting. A study on the kinematics of forgery showed that both reaction time and movement time were significantly slower during simulation conditions (Van Galen & Van Gemmert, 1996). The slower starting time or reaction time can be seen in the static trace through blunt strokes or resting points, which result in a blob of ink during the initial movement of the starting stroke (Huber & Headrick, 1999; Saudek, 1978). The slow duration or movement time is seen in the static trace through the drawn quality of the writing stroke.

These findings are supported by Sita and Rogers (1999), who calculated the mean velocity for the normal writing condition at 4.82 cm/s while the simulating condition was 2.92 cm/s. When analyzing the noise in the power spectral density function contained in the velocity signal, Van Galen & Van Gemmert (1996) found that "forging led to an increase of relative energy in the bands at the lower end of the power spectral density function...the decrease of energy in the tremor-related bands and the increase of high frequency noise is seen as corroboration of the view that forging tasks induce an enhanced limb stiffness in the subject" (p. 19). Harralson et al. (2008) found that in a normal writing condition, the average writer's duration was 6.83 s while the duration during a simulation or forgery condition was 25.52 s, nearly four times longer than the normal writing condition. Similar results were found for velocity with the normal writing condition averaging 3.74 cm/s while the forgery condition was 1.46 cm/s.

Found et al. (1999a) reported that many types of spatial errors occur in forgeries especially in the width of the handwriting, and theorize that "this does tend to make sense in that forgers, when drawing out the line, do so in a serial way" (p. 95). According to Thomassen & Van Galen (1997) "forgery in handwriting imposes specific processing demands (stress) on the motor system...these demands are not necessarily reflected by the spatial features of the finished product, but are expected to become manifest in the kinematics and dynamics of the movements" (p. 97). In the Van Galen & Van Gemmert (1996) study, it was found that "in the spatial domain, the static product of the copies successfully mimicked the original samples" (p. 11). Horan (as cited in Huber & Headrick, 1999) reported that forgeries tend to increase in size. Harralson et al. (2008) found that forgers changed their writing size to match the size of the handwriting they were imitating. Further, when simulating the micrographia of PD handwriting, forgers significantly decreased their own handwriting size.

Results from kinematic handwriting experiments indicate that some characteristics of forgery can be determined from the static trace, and that these characteristics and the observations from handwriting examiners are supportable based upon recent research using quantitative methods with the digital tablet and handwriting capturing software. Evaluating the signs of forgery from the static trace, Hilton (1993) states that "hesitation, unnatural pen lifts, patching, tremor, uncertainty of movement as portrayed by abrupt changes in the direction of the line, and a stilted, drawn quality devoid of free, normal writing movements combine to reveal the true nature of a forgery" (p. 185). Saudek (1978) provides the following signs of spurious handwriting: "slow speed of execution, the subsequent 'touching-up' of individual letters, a frequent change of hold, wavering, uncertain and interrupted strokes of the pen, and marked variations of the angle of writing" (p. 30–31). A comparison of the results found in kinematic research and the characteristics of forgery supplied by Hilton and Saudek indicates that inferences can be made between kinematical and static trace features. Halder-Sinn & Funsch (1998) found that "the high level of the correlation between tremor and speed is surprising, since it was not an objectively recorded parameter but instead was a rating based on a visual inspection of the written trace" (p. 12) (Fig. 3.7).

3.5 HANDWRITING AND DISGUISE

Disguised handwriting can complicate the process of differentiating between genuine and forged writing. Disguise is the process by which a genuine writer changes or alters his or her own handwriting so that it does not resemble the writer's normal handwriting. Sometimes the writer uses their nondominant hand to produce the disguised handwriting sample. Another type of disguise strategy involves autosimulation, in which the genuine writer alters their own handwriting in a subtle way

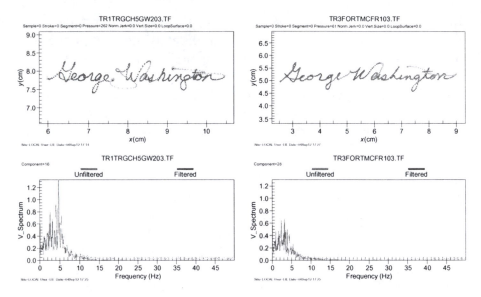

Fig. 3.7 A genuine signature and its velocity frequency spectrum (left) compared to a practiced forgery and its velocity frequency spectrum (right). The peak velocity of the forgery is significantly less than the peak velocity of the genuine writing.

so that it somewhat resembles their natural writing but has some characteristic or detail that is different from their normal writing, which the writer can point out later, in order to claim not to have produced that writing.

Research attention has been directed to special problem areas in handwriting examination such as disguise. It has been recognized in published research on handwriting examiner proficiency testing that evaluating disguise between genuine and forged writing samples increases a handwriting examiner's number of misleading and inconclusive opinions. It was found that in comparison to laypersons, handwriting examiners had lower misleading rates but higher inconclusive rates, indicating the handwriting examiners' conservative approach when expressing opinions on problematic areas such as disguise (Bird et al., 2010a). Another study found that handwriting examiners are correct in detecting that there is a problem with disguised signatures, but that the misleading opinion is a result of attributing incorrect authorship (Bird et al., 2010b).

A study examining differences between genuine, disguised, and autosimulated signatures was conducted using electronic signature technology, so that dynamic handwriting features of each signature could be captured for evaluation and comparison (Mohammed et al.,

Fig. 3.8 Genuine signature (left) compared to disguised signature written with nondominant hand (right).

2011). The disguise study collected 1800 signature samples of different types of signatures that were printed, cursive, or mixed in style. The subjects were asked to provide examples of genuine, disguised, and autosimulated samples that were then measured using handwriting movement capturing software. The handwriting factors examined included duration, size, velocity, jerk, and pen pressure. It was found that changes in handwriting factors were dependent on the style used, and that changes in handwriting velocity and size were caused by the writer's change in handwriting style during a disguise strategy. These types of studies are important in establishing a foundation as to what handwriting examiners may infer from the static trace, but online handwriting studies also help to establish a profile for signature types or strategies that can be expected in the handwriting when it is written online. This data can then be used to improve the accuracy of automatic signature verification systems in addition to training document examiners in detecting disguise (Fig. 3.8).

3.6 HANDWRITING AND NEURO-TECHNOLOGY

Experimental research does not exclusively involve digital tablets and handwriting capturing software. Other innovations have allowed us novel ways of understanding handwriting processes or of capturing and utilizing handwriting movement. Neuro-technology allows us to use instruments to understand the brain in relationship to handwriting movement.

Experimental eye-tracking studies are giving us clues in understanding what a handwriting expert actually observes when examining handwriting in comparison with what a layperson observes. As it has been established that handwriting experts outperform laypersons in proficiency testing, it would be helpful to know the characteristics a handwriting expert observes in handwriting, and how long the expert observes handwriting features, in comparison to laypersons. One experimental eye-tracking study showed that handwriting experts use different cognitive processes than laypersons in evaluating handwriting (Dyer et al.,

2008). Another eye-tracking study found that handwriting experts spend more time examining model signatures than forged signatures, and that genuine signatures with a higher degree of complexity also had longer observation times than signatures with low complexity (Pepe et al., 2011). These studies may have future relevance in helping to develop technology that can be linked to the computer in evaluating handwriting, especially in programming advanced computer systems that can evaluate handwriting samples similar to the way a human examiner evaluates handwriting.

The automated signing of letters or signatures is based on a technology involving the autopen. The autopen is not a new device, as even Thomas Jefferson in the early 1800s used a device similar to the autopen to sign his letters. One of the first autopen devices was developed in 1803 and was similar to a polygraph, while the more modern autopen was developed in the 1930s. Now, the autopen device has been updated with computer technology to include flash memory drives, smart cards, security features, and liquid crystal display screens. Automated Signature Technology (2011) produces a machine that works with a card (similar to a credit card) containing an image of the signature. The card is inserted into the device, and then a pen connected to metal arms reproduces the signature image onto the page. Autopen devices are used in autograph signing and mass mailing to personalize the signature without the need for the original signer spending hours signing hundreds of documents. While the autopen produces signatures that accurately capture the static features of the handwriting, close examination of these signatures reveals line quality characteristics associated with slowly drawn writing movement, such as blunt endings and overly even pressure patterns. Typically, these types of signatures can be differentiated from handwritten simulations because the handwriting line quality features have a mechanical and overly consistent pressure pattern. Additionally, the autopen replicates a signature pattern so there is no natural range of variation in these types of mechanically produced signatures which could also help distinguish them from both genuine writing samples and freehand simulations.

Developments in neuro-engineering are producing technology that mimics not only the static features of the handwriting but its fluency and movement (Kulvicius et al., 2012). A robotic arm was engineered using a combination of neuro-technology and computational neuroscience which helped develop fluid and smooth movements in the robot arm that can simulate handwriting movement. The engineers found that producing smooth movement was challenging due to the complex movement patterns in handwriting that involve joining handwriting trajectories. The technology can produce accurate movements in both position and velocity with fluency, or in simpler terms, the robotic arm can mimic the form features of the handwriting as well as the speed features of the movement.

Besides kinematical studies, electromyographic (EMG) signals are used to recreate handwriting movement (Linderman et al., 2009). The EMG signals are taken not from the handwriting but from hand and forearm muscles; algorithms are used to recreate the handwriting traces or to select font characters (based on the signal) in order to translate the handwriting into typed text. The EMG signal may have useful information about clinical conditions that may not be detectable from traditional kinematic approaches (such as digital tablets). This technology may be useful for computerized technology and prosthetic devices, as well as for diagnostic purposes in understanding handwriting impairment in Parkinson's, Alzheimer's, and ADHD.

3.7 SUMMARY

Advances in the science and technology of capturing handwriting movements, also known as handwriting kinematics, have been exploited in the medical field. The extensive research into motor movement using handwriting capturing technology has contributed extensively to knowledge about handwriting variability that can occur in unusual or health-related conditions. A greater understanding of movement disorders such as PD and ET has been gained through analysis of handwriting movement. Handwriting kinematics has also aided in our understanding of how certain psychiatric disorders influence the motor system. Clinicians can now use handwriting movement measurements to make adjustments to psychiatric patient medications. The effects of alcohol, caffeine, and sleep deprivation on handwriting movement have also been demonstrated through kinematics research. The knowledge gained from the medical field about handwriting kinematics has been used to further study the effects of forgery and disguise in handwriting. Advances in handwriting neuro-technology has aided in our understanding of how handwriting examiners cognitively process signatures while new technology has produced a sophisticated robotic arm that can mimic the dynamic movement of natural handwriting.

CHAPTER 4

Digital and Electronic Handwriting

In 2000, a bill was passed in the United States making digital signatures as legally binding to contracts as manuscript signatures written with an ink pen on paper. Other countries already had similar litigation or have followed suit, and now digital signatures are in widespread use internationally. What exactly constitutes a "digital signature" is broad in scope, and the terminology for this new and evolving type of signature has caused confusion even among forensic experts. Because there is variance in terminology relating to digital, electronic, and biometric signatures, this section will attempt to clarify (and perhaps help to standardize) terminology. In addition, a glossary focusing on digital handwriting technology is provided at the end of the book.

Because this book focuses on handwriting examination, we will introduce what is typically referred to as a "digital signature." However, the discussion will emphasize what we will refer to as "electronic signatures" or "biometric signatures" which are handwritten and attached to a document electronically, unlike digital signatures which are computerized algorithms and have little in common with a manuscript signature.

4.1 THE ELECTRONIC SIGNATURE ACT

The Electronic Signatures in Global and National Commerce Act of 2000 specifies a general rule of validity with respect to electronic signatures: "a signature, contract, or other record relating to such transaction may not be denied legal effect, validity, or enforceability because it is in electronic form." Effectively, the law makes e-signatures as enforceable and valid as traditional manuscript signatures.

Interestingly, the law does state that it does not "require any person to agree to use or accept electronic records or electronic signatures." The Act specifies the consumer's rights to have access to electronic records upon request and the right of the consumer to have a record made available in nonelectronic form. The consumer also is to be provided with a statement about the hardware and software requirements needed for control and access of electronic records prior to signing.

There has been an attempt to define a digital or electronic signature and to understand comprehensively what an electronic signature may represent from a legal perspective. The Act provides several definitions for terms used throughout the document. Specifically, "electronic signature" is defined as "an electronic sound, symbol, or process, attached to or logically associated with a contract or other record and executed or adopted by a person with the intent to sign the record." This definition clearly shows the broad use of the term "electronic signature", which could be an algorithm-based digital signature or an electronically captured handwritten signature, and does not distinguish between these two types of electronic signatures.

The European Union passed a similar Act in 1999 that pre-dated the United States' 2000 Act with basically the same provisions: that the legality of a signature could not be denied if it is electronic in nature. Mason (2010), in a review of electronic signatures globally, found that "there is no specific provision for the concept of an advanced electronic signature in the Act" (p. 331). Mason sets forth that a signature is an intentional act that encompasses not only ink on paper but also includes wax seals as a type of signature. As such, Mason specifies several intents that can be construed as electronic signatures: typing a name onto a document, an e-mail address, clicking an "I accept" icon, a personal identification number (PIN), a biodynamic signature, a scanned signature, and a digital signature. According to Mason, "a bio-dynamic signature of a manuscript signature uses a special pen and pad measure and records the action of the person as they sign. This creates a digital version of the manuscript signature" (Ibid., p. 333).

4.2 APPLICATIONS FOR ELECTRONIC SIGNATURES

The applications for electronic signature technology are extensive, and they are in widespread use at an international level. Biometric signature software and hardware is manufactured and marketed by major corporations to areas such as finance, banking, health care, and mortgage lenders. Electronic signatures are used for access control, network access control, client identification purposes, document workflows, and electronic transaction security. Since the enactment of electronic signature legislation, the use of digital and other forms of electronic signatures has increased significantly. They are used for contractual agreements, delivery verification, biometric security checkpoints, bank signature cards, and point-of-sale transactions. Traditional business has incorporated them into use for contractual negotiations, even in conservative business markets. Online signature verification system corporations have targeted large corporations to incorporate their products into their business systems. Corporations are also marketing to small businesses, indicating that usage of online signature systems is expanding.

The apparent ease and convenience with which a document can now be signed using electronic signature technology makes e-signatures popular in spite of potential authentication and legal problems that can be associated with e-signatures. Companies marketing electronic signature technology point out that e-signatures eliminate faxes, phone calls, and next day delivery services, while saving time spent tracking down documents trying to get them signed. There is less paper involved, and documents can be signed in minutes by all parties. Of course, little is made of the mishaps that can occur with e-signatures. When the technology does not work, either through computer or human error, or through lack of access to technology, more time can be wasted trying to get the technology to work than would have been used in relying on traditional signing methods.

It is inevitable that the use of various forms of electronic signature technology will increase internationally as it maintains popularity and social acceptability as opposed to comparable forms of biometric analysis. Because signatures are intuitively associated with identity and are unique to the individual, they are more user-friendly, less invasive, and more natural than other forms of biometric identification such as fingerprint, iris, facial, and gait recognition.

There are advocates for passwords, PINs, and smart cards as replacements for the signature even claiming that they are more secure. Some believe biometric identification is better because biometric analysis identifies a person; it is not about the knowledge someone may have, which can be easily shared with others. Cards and passwords can be stolen or shared; they do not provide identity, and such information is easily compromised. Biometrics provide information as to the identity of the person, and are more resistant to alteration and reverse engineering which can occur with smart cards and chip and PIN technology. Biometrics also provide more security against identity theft.

This is not to say that biometrics is without problems of security and identification. There are drawbacks to some forms of biometrics, especially physiological biometrics that identify finger or hand prints, iris, or DNA. KeCrypt Systems Ltd. (2012) reports how a head cold can cause a false negative in an iris scan, while a latent print can be lifted and used for a fingerprint to gain access. Other biometrics such as gait, voice, and handwriting are behavioral and subject to variability, but cannot be exactly replicated. The problems with physiological biometrics are so well known that they are even referred to in popular films and television, sometimes in gruesome ways, such as the dismemberment of a finger to access a biometric fingerprint scan. Unfortunately, these types of cases are real as a finger dismemberment case was reported by Mason (2010). In that case, the victim's fingers were cut off by the thief in order to start the victim's car that was equipped with a fingerprint sensor. Wide public exposure to the failure of a high-tech biometric system, dramatically and convincingly presented in a way that shows exactly how such a system can be cracked, is not likely to increase public confidence in the use of biometrics.

Signatures do not have the same problems associated with fingerprints because fingerprints are replicable, while signatures are different every time a person signs. So, rather than identifying an exact match (as is the case with iris scans and fingerprint scans), signatures are examined for temporal-based patterns. An exact match would indicate to the expert or verification systems that the signature has been replicated, resulting in a rejection of the signature. Like fingerprint and iris scans, though, signatures also have identification problems—principally due to their varying nature. Natural handwriting variation, health issues, and other variables can cause changes to the signature, leading to possible false negatives.

In the final analysis, digital signature technology is not living up to its claim of making signatures more secure. The primary advantage to digital signature technology is that it makes signing easier in a digitized world. Therefore, the popularity of digital signatures is fundamentally for convenience, not for improved security. The most important challenge facing digital and electronic signatures is making the signature secure in a digital environment.

4.3 SECURITY AND PRIVACY ISSUES

Although nearly all handwriting and signature systems available on the market claim that their products provide security, a review of some of the basic features of these systems calls into question not only the level of security but even the ability of forensic investigators, either document examiners or computer experts, to prove the identity of the person signing. For example, one electronic signature system available on the market has signers select a font version of their signature, which is then embedded into the document, using digital signature cryptography. The security of this system is dependent upon identifying the computer in which the signature is selected, as there is no real signature to examine either in digitized form or through online capture. If there was a future question as to the authenticity of the document, the security features examined would be dependent on identifying the computer on which the signature was signed. That investigation can help eliminate most suspected signers—unless the computer was stolen or the signature was produced on a public computer. Additionally, since many suspect signature cases are disputes between couples or families, anyone (such as a spouse) with access to private information could sign for the other spouse much more easily than attempting to forge the spouse's pen and ink signature. While a sophisticated biometric signing system can certainly help secure one's signature, many e-signing systems do not use biometric signature data.

Protecting one's signature in our digital society is at a disadvantage concerning privacy issues as well. This is highlighted in legal complaints that originated in Canada concerning the unauthorized publication of delivery signatures on a courier service's web site (Mason, 2012). It was common practice for the courier service to capture a signature on an electronic device upon delivery. The e-signatures were then published on its web site along with the shipping and tracking information related to the delivered parcels. The first complainant refused to sign on the electronic signature device, requesting to sign a paper receipt instead. He was denied this option and compelled to sign on the electronic device. The second complainant discovered that his signature had been published on the web site and requested that it be removed; the courier service denied his request. The U.S. Postal Service also digitizes signatures on delivery confirmation forms and posts them on its Internet web site where anyone with a delivery confirmation number can type the number into the U.S. Postal Service web site and view a digitized image of the signer's signature. It is expected that privacy issues will become more of a concern as electronic signatures are published on the Internet, frequently without consent.

4.4 DIGITAL TECHNOLOGY

In order to analyze a signature digitally, we need a greater understanding of the technology behind digitization. In our modern, computerized world, digital technology has revolutionized images in television, film, music, and photography. While advances in digitization of signatures has allowed us to digitize our signature when writing a signature on a digital tablet, digitization of signatures has been occurring for several years through scanning, facsimile, and photography of documents.

The process of digitization involves the conversion of information (such as documents) into bits or bytes. These bits are points or samples of information. The higher the number of bits, the higher the resolution and closer approximation the digital process has to the analog signal. Resolution is typically measured in pixels. There are two primary ways of acquiring digital information. With handwriting, the digital signature can be scanned from a source document. Or the signature can be captured using a digital device such as a tablet and stylus. Special software can be involved in capturing the signature digitally, or, the tablet and stylus serve as a replacement for a mouse and the signature can be drawn and captured onto the computer screen.

On some digital tablet surfaces with an active display, the user can see the signature or drawing as it is produced on the surface of the tablet in real time or near real time (as some active displays may lag behind real time). The writing appearing on the active display is referred to as "digital ink." Digital ink helps to create a more natural signing environment where the signer can see the signature being written in real time on the display. "Through this technology, the quality of both the enrollments and the verifications can be considered relatively high. The quality of forgeries additionally also improves by this technique, since dealing with the active displays corresponds to the natural human writing behavior" (Scheidat et al., 2006, p. 187).

Although much of the research from the 1980s focused on handwriting movement recordings for health issues, this research also led to experiments involving examination of natural versus forged handwriting movement (Van Galen & Van Gemmert, 1996). Digital tablet recording allows for the capture of handwriting movements in the x and y coordinates (horizontal and vertical dimensions). Other factors frequently measured include dynamic, time-based coordinates such as velocity and duration. Sophisticated software programs that record handwriting from digital tablets for experimental research have included OASIS and NeuroScript MovAlyzeR.

In research by Teulings & Maarse (1984), the researchers commented that "digitizers are designed to transmit to a digital computer single pairs of horizontal and vertical coordinates of the current position specified by a cross-hair cursor or by the tip of a stylus" (p. 194). The horizontal and vertical positions need to be sampled simultaneously. The transmitted information sends both static and dynamic information to the computer for processing. During sampling and preprocessing, samples may be inserted in order to maintain continuity. Inserting samples is necessary when the pen is lifted high (e.g., 1 cm) because the tablet will then suspend capturing the pen tip position until the pen is lowered near the tablet again. Linear interpolation is used to approximate the value of the coordinates based upon the x and y coordinates. In simple terms, interpolation is used to fill gaps where known samples or quantities may not be known, but it is an educated guess based on the location of the known samples in relationship to each other. Time stamps are taken for each sample to ensure that the interpolated samples equate to the duration of the pen lift.

Samples are also altered or "smoothed" to reduce the effects of noise. The noise is caused by disturbances of the stylus on the surface of the tablet which is referred to as "white noise." There is also "quantization noise" involving the conversion of an analog signal to a discrete, digital signal with a limited number of bits. To lessen the noise of the signal, a process called low-pass filtering is employed, which is possible when using higher-than-necessary sampling frequencies: oversampling can compensate for the problems involved with a noisy signal. High sampling rates and low-pass digital filters are used to deal with the informational "noise"—distortion of data—that is produced by the operation of the equipment itself, as well as to deal with analog-to-digital conversion. This is particularly important when the signal-to-noise ratio (i.e., the ratio between the amplitude of the movement divided by the amplitude of the noise) is low.

Fast Fourier Transform "applied to the handwriting signal (which has been made cyclic) yields a (complex) frequency spectrum" (Teulings & Maarse, 1984, p. 204). This frequency spectrum allows for an analysis of the signal and shows the filtered noise throughout the entire frequency spectrum but the movement in the low-frequency bandwidth is about 10 Hz. Besides horizontal and vertical position, relevant time functions in motor research are horizontal and vertical velocity (i.e., the first time derivative), absolute velocity or speed (i.e., magnitude of the velocity vector irrespective of direction), and horizontal and vertical acceleration (i.e., the second time derivative).

Time derivatives (such as velocity, acceleration, and jerk) are calculated from the handwriting position as a function of time by estimating the rate of change with time once, twice, or thrice, respectively. Segmentation into up and downstrokes is done by finding zero crossings in the vertical velocity. For finding the exact zero crossing, linear interpolation is employed to correct for the discrete sampling frequency.

For example, the derivative of position versus time is velocity. By repeating the estimation of the rate of change we obtain higher derivatives. The second derivative of position as a function of time is acceleration and the third derivative is jerk.

4.5 DIGITAL AND ELECTRONIC SIGNATURES

Digitization of a signature is quite a different process from what is popularly referred to as a "digital signature." The nomenclature in the area of digital signatures is confusing and can potentially lead to communication problems in explanations in court rooms to judges or juries. One of the goals of this text is to help clarify some of the issues concerning definitions in the field.

A digital signature in computer security terms refers to an algorithm-based, computer-encoded "signature." This type of "signature" is comprised of encrypted computer code and has no resemblance in process or product to a manuscript signature written on a digital tablet (which is known as an electronic or biometric signature). A digital signature is a secure mathematical formula that is encrypted so that the receiver of the document knows that the document has been sent by the intended sender. The National Institute of Standards and Technology (NIST) defines a digital signature as "an electronic analogue of a written signature" (2009, p. 9).

There are three parts to the digital signature process, which include signature generation using an algorithm that issues a key pair, a private key and a public key. The "signature" that is generated is attached to a compressed digest message through a hash function along with the private key. The hash function creates a digital fingerprint or condensed version of the document. Signature verification is performed through the match between the sender's private key and the receiver's public key. Once a document is digitally signed, it is not possible to change or alter the contents of the document, so digital signatures help to authenticate the contents of a document and provide security measures so that documents are not altered after they are digitally signed.

Nonrepudiation of a digital signature refers to the inability of the entity in possession of the public key to deny having signed the document. Although it is claimed that digital signatures provide more security and are harder to forge than manually signed signatures (either on tablets or paper), they have different types of weaknesses that render them vulnerable to the same weaknesses inherent in password- and PIN-protected systems. For example, the security of the digital signature is dependent upon access to the private key. If the computer where the private key is stored is not secure, this makes the private key vulnerable. It may not be possible to conclusively determine the identity of the person with access to the private key if the private key's password has been shared or its security has in some way been compromised. There are levels of protection to secure private keys to make them less vulnerable to theft or hacking, and also to make them transportable so that the private key can be used on other computers. Private keys can be stored on smart cards with embedded security features so that even if the smart card were stolen, the private key could not be used because it is protected by a PIN or password.

In spite of these security features, it is important to note that digital signatures do not conclusively prove the identity of the signer. Bechini (2009) points out that "a manuscript signature links a document to a person, while a digital signature does not: it links a document to a device" (p. 80). Mason (2010) points out that a digital signature is only as secure as the password that protects it. Passwords do not identify the person at either end of the digital signing process, as passwords can be shared and stolen.

A digitized signature, or electronically captured signature, is one in which the signer employs conventional methods in physically signing a signature, except instead of using traditional ink and paper, the signer writes on a tablet or screen with a stylus or fingertip. This type of signature is also referred to as a biometric or biodynamic signature, which is recorded using online handwriting capturing methods that record not only the spatial properties of a signature but also temporal characteristics such as the velocity and duration measurements. Capturing a signature "online" refers to recording the handwriting movement in real time, usually on a digital tablet (Fig. 4.1).

A digitized signature could also refer to a pen and ink signature that has been scanned or faxed and thereby "digitized" for purposes of storage, capture, or even handwriting verification. Scanned handwriting is also used in handwriting recognition software. These types of signatures are also referred to as offline signatures, because the static image of the signature is digitized with no biodynamic information available.

Digital and electronic signatures are sometimes used together to secure an electronically captured handwritten signature onto a

Fig. 4.1 Comparison of a traditional ink and paper signature (top) with a digitized tablet signature (bottom).

document. Some systems use both the digital and electronic signature together, while other systems employ only the electronic signature.

4.6 DIGITIZATION OF SIGNATURES: OPTICAL SCANNING AND FACSIMILE

Digitization of handwriting or signatures involves scanning and facsimile. The quality of the signature is dependent upon the resolution quality of the scan, measurable in dots per inch (dpi). Low resolution will cause the signature to produce a pixelized or digitized effect that can make the line quality of the signature appear ragged. Higher resolution will reduce the pixelized look, but under high enough magnification, pixels are observed instead of the characteristics of the ink line quality (Figs 4.2 and 4.3).

Digitization is also seen in digital photography of signatures in addition to electronically captured signatures. In order to smooth the line quality of enlarged images, a digital processing feature such as interpolation is used. When there is a known set of captured data points, as frequently found in electronically captured signatures, further processing can be achieved through interpolation. Rather than gathering 200 sample points per second, 100 sample points can be gathered, and interpolation is used to fill in the gaps. In mathematics, regression

Fig. 4.2 High-resolution scan (left) and low-resolution scan (right).

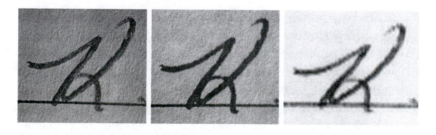

Fig. 4.3 Magnified ink image (left). Magnified copy machine toner image (middle). Enlarged scan image (right).

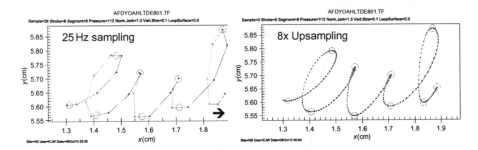

Fig. 4.4 Example of interpolation. Handwriting sample captured at 25 Hz is upsampled to 200 Hz.

analysis or curve fitting is used to construct new data points between the range of known data points (Fig. 4.4).

Interpolation is also used in digital photography, particularly in optical zoom features which fill in the gaps between points of digital data when enlarging the image. Some scanner software also uses interpolation.

4.7 DIGITAL TABLETS

The digital tablet is an important component in the capture of digitized signatures. Some rudimentary form of electronic tablet has existed since the late 1800s, but tablets became more practical and popular with advancements in Computer-Aided Drafting and Design (CADD) and used in AutoCADD systems as early as the 1970s. Tablets for personal computers with handwriting recognition technology started to become available in the 1980s. Research in the electronic capture of handwriting using digital tablets was also conducted in the 1980s, especially with the onset of a variety of digital tablet devices that made capture of handwriting movement recordings easier.

There are ever-growing numbers of devices involved with signature and handwriting capture including tablet PCs, personal digital assistants (PDAs), mobile telephones, and other devices. The different tablet devices available on the market can impact the handwriting signal significantly. Commercially available tablets manufactured by Wacom Co., Ltd., and used extensively in handwriting research, rely on electromagnetic induction to transmit and receive information to and from the stylus. The stylus also contains electronics for receiving and transmitting information. These signals help establish the position of the stylus on the tablet. Other tablets that exclusively receive information from the stylus can result in less white noise in the signal. Alonso-Fernandez et al. (2005) found that the tablet can make a difference in performance. For example, in a handwriting verification experiment, the researchers found that certain tablets perform better due to sampling frequency oscillation.

Tablets are able to receive signal information from the stylus without the stylus touching the tablet. This helps in determining the location of the stylus above the tablet (known as pen position), pen tilt, and x and y positions on the tablet. One of the characteristics analyzed from the information above the tablet surface involves air strokes (the strokes produced in the air when a person is breaking between letters or words and creates a pen lift). Some of the unique handwriting features captured by the digitization of signatures allows for novel methods in forensic detection (explored in Chapter 5).

Touch pads or touch screens are also used for producing signatures. Some devices allow for writing with both the stylus and the touch pad interchangeably. The touch pad is pressure-sensitive to the fingertip. Research has shown that there are user performance differences in point-selected tasks between the touch pad and the mouse (Akamatsu & MacKenzie, 2002). An advantage for the touch pad is convenience. The touch pad, along with one's fingertip, is all that is needed for signing one's signature. No additional devices, such as stylus or mouse, are necessary. This technology increases convenience and allows for signing signatures on laptop computers, tablet computers, and cell phones. Point-of-sale signatures using a touch pad–based cell phone connected to a credit card capturing device are presently used.

Convenience is a primary factor for the popularity and widespread use of touch pad-based signatures, but the physical limitations of these signatures do not allow for handwriting precision. Research into touch pads has shown that error rates are a problem when the device is held in the hand, but the errors are also due to the small size of the strokes in comparison to the width of the fingertip (Isokoski & Kaki, 2002). Handwriting was developed using fine-tipped writing instruments like quills, fountain pens, ballpoint pens, and the stylus. The breadth of the fingertip in writing small, narrow movements diminishes the precision in the fine detail of the signature.

4.8 THE STYLUS AND OTHER WRITING "INSTRUMENTS"

"Pen computing" is a term used to refer to use of a digital pen or stylus instead of a cursor. The stylus is used in conjunction with digital tablets, tablet PCs, and mobile devices. Electronic ink is the digitized handwriting seen on a digital display and is sometimes converted to print characters using handwriting recognition technology. Not all graphic signatures are captured using a stylus as some systems allow users to use a mouse to sign the signature. There are manufacturers that state that such signatures are forensically reliable, even though using a mouse is highly awkward for the signer. In fact, research has shown that signing with a mouse may render a signature forensically unreliable, especially when it is compared to nonrepresentative samples (Harralson et al., 2011). Signatures can also be signed with the tip of a finger, using a pressure-sensitive touch pad. While this type of signature may allow the writer more control over the fine motor movements than using a mouse, touch pad finger signatures are still more awkward in comparison to signing with a pen on paper or even with a digital pen or stylus.

In order to differentiate "digital ink" from the real ink in pen and paper signatures when discussing electronic signature technology, the term "wet ink" (or "wet signature") has been used to refer to pen ink on paper. There is a considerable volume of research about the analysis of traditional inking pens and paper in forensic document examination literature (Brunelle & Reed, 1984; Brunelle & Crawford, 2003; Causin et al., 2011; Ezcurra, 2012; Lyter, 1982; Samanidou et al., 2007; Senior et al., 2012). The physical attributes of ink pen traces have been extensively examined including the width of the ink-trace, line quality characteristics created by pen nibs and ink, and the micropatterns in inner ink-trace characteristics (Barabe et al., 2003; Brink et al., 2012; Franke, 2005, 2007b). The research into ink-trace characteristics has aided in developing sophisticated offline features for computerized handwriting verification systems.

Computer technology has created new writing instruments, although some make the handwriting task uncomfortable and awkward. Many of the stylus pens used with graphics tablets are constructed similar in shape to a real pen. When the signer holds the stylus, it feels like a pen and allows for natural handwriting movement. Some styluses are outfitted with plastic pen nibs that glide across the surface of the tablet in a slippery way. A sensor within some of the more sophisticated digital pens (such as those produced by Wacom Co., Ltd.) can detect pressure and using pressure on the stylus on the tablet replaces clicking on a mouse. Digital pens are used for graphics design and the pressure applied on the digital pen can draw thick or thin lines depending on the amount of force or pressure used to press down on the digital pen.

Some digital tablet pens use plastic nibs and real ballpoint pen inking nibs interchangeably. Placing a piece of paper over the digital tablet and using the inking version of the tablet pen allows for the capture of the recorded signature while also capturing a hard copy version on paper simultaneously. These types of inking pens are not always common and frequently need to be specially ordered as they are not automatically included with the digital tablet when purchased. They are also more expensive than the typical stylus included with digital tablets.

While the stylus allows for writing a signature with greater detail and precision than writing with a fingertip, not all styluses have the same level of technological sophistication. Especially when signers encounter point-of-sale devices, the stylus can be notoriously bulky and awkward: ill-fitted to the task of producing a detailed and accurate signature. Some are as simple as a plastic stick with a pointed tip, with no associated electronics inside the pen. Some devices that produce "digital ink" on the display (the trace left behind on the surface of some digital tablet displays) have a plastic stylus attached to the pad. Others are the equivalent of writing with what feels like an unsharpened crayon or a stick with a wide tip. There is even a soft stylus with a broad rubber tip that prevents scratching the surface of the display. Some large stylus nibs are not conducive to writing inside small signature-sized tablet boxes. In some instances, the broad stylus is comparatively too large for the small size of the tablet or display associated with the stylus. Some pressure-sensitive pads allow for both a stylus and a fingertip. The same dimension problems also apply between a small tablet or display and a fingertip signing a signature. A fingertip is usually too broad and blunt for the size of the display.

Many tablets can also be used with a mouse. While the thought of signing one's signature with a computer mouse is not particularly intuitive or natural, it is encouraged by some companies that advertise electronic signature technology. Signing a signature with a mouse on a digital tablet probably produces a greater level of accuracy than

Fig. 4.5 Signatures signed with stylus (top), finger (middle), and mouse (bottom).

signing the signature on a desk surface. Usually, signing with a mouse also involves clicking and then moving the mouse next to the computer while watching the movement of the handwriting on the computer screen. This type of signing creates multiple levels of challenge for producing accurate and consistent signatures. The mouse is awkward and does not allow for the traditional "tripod" grip on the pen which allows for maximum manual control in handwriting. Further, watching the writing on a computer screen instead of on a tablet or paper can also seem awkward and unnatural, especially if the writer has problems directing the mouse to sign within a certain field or box on the computer screen. The mouse, just like the stylus, also has differing degrees of accuracy depending on the device (Fig. 4.5).

Use of a tablet or display is not always required for handwriting capture. The digital pen, such as the Dane-Elec Zpen (Dane-Elec Digital Products, 2008), writes on paper with ballpoint pen ink while connected to a receiver that records handwritten notes onto the computer screen. The device can convert handwritten notes into digital text, and it can also interface with handwriting movement software. The Livescribe (2012) Smartpen records audio and handwritten notes using special microdot paper, which enables the infrared camera at the tip of the Smartpen to track everything that is written down.

A novel concept in writing technology that is being currently explored, and one that is all too familiar to children, involves the detection of air writing, using what is referred to as 3D handwriting recognition. Using a hands-free device, a person can write in the air, as though they were writing on an imaginary blackboard. The handwritten material is detected by a motion-sensing device and identified and recognized using a support vector machine and hidden Markov values

(Amma et al., 2012). Experimentation with the 3D handwriting recognition system showed an 11% word error rate.

4.9 HANDWRITING RECOGNITION TECHNOLOGY

Handwriting recognition is the technology used to convert handwritten characters into text-based characters using optical character recognition (OCR). Initially, such technology was used when scanning documents and converting the handwritten characters into text read on a computer screen. However, now handwriting recognition is also used to convert online handwriting into text-based characters. In the first process, the handwriting is considered "offline" meaning that the handwriting is scanned and recognized from static handwriting on a document. "Online" handwriting recognition refers to the conversion of handwriting into text while the person is writing in real time on a tablet.

In handwriting recognition, there are two stages used in the process of OCR, which include handwriting feature extraction and classification. Popular methods used for classification include Artificial Neural Networks (ANNs) and Hidden Markov Values (Sarojini & Sireesha, 2012). Handwriting recognition technology is also used in handwriting identification research. An example of such research involves the application of a system originally intended as a handwriting recognition system, used by the U.S. Postal Service for reading postal addresses. This system was used in an experiment that proved the individuality of handwriting (Srihari et al., 2002). Aside from signature and document authentication and verification, handwriting recognition is also used for check processing in banks, address recognition, and research of historical documents.

4.10 AUTOMATED FORENSIC HANDWRITING ANALYSIS TECHNOLOGY

The computerized and automated identification and verification of handwriting is based upon many of the computerized methods that originated in handwriting recognition technology. Srihari et al. (2002) explain the fundamental difference between handwriting recognition and handwriting identification technology: handwriting recognition filters out individuality in order to capture the common elements of handwriting, in order to convert it to text, or in searching for a particular word that may be common between samples or writers. Handwriting identification is focused on exactly the opposite, as its intent is to capture the individuality and uniqueness of handwriting and how that individuality differentiates it from other samples that employ the same handwritten letters or text. Handwriting verification systems also employ mathematical and statistical formulas for comparison and matching of handwriting in a database to establish identification.

The Forensic Information System for Handwriting (FISH) was designed to help automatize the document examination process and increase efficiency through the computerized ability to scan, digitize, measure, store, and compare questioned and known handwriting samples. FISH measurements include letter characteristics such as height and distance of letters. WANDA, designed to interface with FISH, has advanced features, including additional handwriting measurements and modules that represent systematic handwriting examination procedures (Franke et al., 2004). The first procedure includes data acquisition which is the capture of handwriting through offline methods (such as scanning) or online methods (digital tablet input). Preprocessing involves the removal of data that can interfere with feature extraction and analysis (such as lines, backgrounds, color, and other graphic features that can affect feature analysis). The annotation of handwritten elements labels or identifies attributes and values of components of the document or text (e.g., the language of the document, nature of the document, and style of the handwriting). The measurement module is based on pattern-recognition techniques that aid in the development of adding a measurement for allograph matching. The measurements include height, slant, and width of characters and baseline measurements. Automatic feature extraction is based on the premise that it is the combination of unique characteristics that establishes handwriting identification; one feature alone is not sufficient to establish identification.

A significant study (mentioned earlier) that established the individuality of handwriting in forensic identification employed an automated system that was originally invented for postal address handwriting recognition (Srihari et al., 2002). This study published a detailed explanation of the underlying process generally used by automated handwriting systems. In the study, the three phases of the automated analysis included handwriting data collection, feature extraction, and validation to establish a statistical model for handwriting identification. For data collection, samples of representative types of handwritings were used to build a 1500 sample handwriting database. In the feature extraction phase, the handwriting samples were scanned and converted into binary (black and white) samples. Adobe Photoshop was used for segmentation and extraction of line, word, and character images.

In the feature extraction phase, features were identified as quantitative measurements from different levels of the handwriting exaction phase. The features were measured from the samples and feature vectors developed. Several features were extracted for study including conventional features that are observable by human document examiners and computational features which are extracted and normalized using computer algorithms.

For statistical analysis, an ANN was employed in the study. ANNs are mathematical or computational models that are used to model relationships and find patterns in data. ANN is based on machine learning and artificial intelligence, useful for data mining and pattern-based analysis. ANN also works well with Bayesian procedures, an increasingly used statistical method for determining probability in forensic analysis. In the study, an ANN was trained to examine within-writer and between-writer variances at the document, paragraph, word, and character levels. The data was analyzed for identification of a writer against other writers (identification), as well as for comparing the writing of a document to another writing to verify that it is written by the same person (verification). Results showed that the system had a 98% accuracy rate for identification and a 96% accuracy rate for verification. The high performance of the system's method was based on just a few macro- and microfeatures, but the authors pointed out that such identification or verification could not be determined by a single feature, indicating that handwriting identification and verification is dependent upon a set of features. Additionally, the results were based upon features that are used by document examiners, as well as on features that are computationally based, suggesting that computers can provide statistical analysis and inference that is not possible with the more traditional methods of handwriting examination.

Driven by the development of biometric systems, advancement in automated forensic handwriting analysis includes online feature analysis and sophisticated algorithms. There are intelligent systems that extract both offline and online features as well as what is referred to as global and local features. Global features are associated with signature "properties as a whole," while local features refer to "properties specific to a sampling point" (Tariq et al., 2011, p. 11). The forensic applicability and discriminatory value of specific global and local features in online and offline handwriting feature extraction is reviewed in Chapter 5, including the forensic performance of automated handwriting analysis systems.

Algorithms such as Dynamic Time Warping (DTW) are used in online handwriting and signature systems, which match handwriting samples using temporal and spatial characteristics captured in real time. Niels & Vuurpijl (2005) describe DTW in handwriting examination as a "technique that compares online trajectories of coordinates (i.e., trajectories in which both spatial and temporal information is available)" (p. 218). DTW can be described as following two similar writing patterns, and moving the "time" forward at variable rates so that the writing patterns will be at the same "time" at corresponding turning and reversal points. DTW is useful in comparing the similarity in the sequence between two handwriting units or samples even if they are produced in different time lengths. This technique would be particularly useful in online handwriting systems.

The Hidden Markov Model (HMM) is another algorithm that is used in both online and offline systems for sequence modeling in handwriting. This algorithm helps to process handwriting data not as single allographs or units but as sequences of letters. The algorithm predicts stroke sequence: the stroke that follows next depends on the preceding stroke. For example, after an upstroke is produced, the chance of a downstroke is very high. HMM is especially useful for temporal pattern recognition where the output of the handwriting pattern is recognizable but the process of the handwriting is not known. The HMM provides information about sequence when modeling handwriting and is used in automatic signature verification (Kashi et al., 1997).

A Gaussian Mixture Model (GMM) "is a parametric probability density function represented as a weighted sum of Gaussian component densities. GMMs are commonly used as a parametric model of the probability distribution of continuous measurements or features in a biometric system" (Reynolds, 2008). GMMs are also used in handwriting verification systems, sometimes in conjunction with HMMs.

Gannon Technologies Group has developed what is referred to and trademarked as Graph-based Recognition Technology, a technique similar to isomorphic graph matching. While Gannon is partially relying on traditional handwriting recognition techniques, it has further developed a method for handwriting identification that is biometric in nature. Handwriting-derived biometric identification is enabled through the use of recognizing and associating each graph element in a body of writing to an alphabet letter (Gantz et al., 2005). Because each graph may involve the calculating of hundreds of measurements, Gannon has developed a technique called the Biometric Kernel that reduces the measurements to the ones that are biometrically unique or identifiable to the writer. The so-called Biometric Kernel of that writer is then used to compare to the other writing samples in the database to locate other possible matches in the database. The technology extends to cursive elements, or pictographs, in connected handwriting as well as the ability to recognize connected parts of text graphically instead of isolating parts exclusively to a single alphabetical unit (Walch & Gantz, 2004).

4.11 STANDARDIZATION

The NIST (2009) published a digital signature standard which defines a digital signature and specifies the minimum requirements for digital signature technology. The NIST digital signature standard, at over 100 pages in length, provides technical specifics concerning the minimum security and quality requirements necessary in the creation of digital signatures. The International Organization for Standardization (ISO) has developed a standard on what is termed "Biometric data interchange formats" (ISO/IEC 19794:2007). The standard provides specifics regarding data interchange formats for temporal, behavioral handwriting data captured on digital tablets or pen systems.

BioAPI 2.0 (Biometric Application Programming Interface) defines a standardized interface for using biometric devices, algorithms, and archives within systems for enrollment and verification. BioAPI allows for software from multiple software systems to work under one protocol. In Europe, a central Biometric Matching System (BMS) has been implemented which uses software created by Daon (2011).

While standards on digital, electronic, and biometric signatures exist, the real problem is the enforcement of the standards in an industry whose focus may be on cost and convenience over security. Suppliers are merely meeting the demands of the consumer who may assume security from systems, but is more motivated by cost and convenience.

While electronic signature technology has satisfied a need for convenience in signing in the global marketplace, standardization of electronic signature technology is a problem, especially in the forensic analysis of disputed handwriting or documents. If manufacturers and users of the technology do not comply with the minimum standards established within the industry, the signature or handwriting produced by this type of technology may be considered forensically unreliable. From a practical standpoint, though, it is doubtful whether the legal system and even forensic examiners are sufficiently aware of the minimum standards and procedures required for capturing and authenticating an electronic signature. This is a critical point, because in forensically evaluating these types of signatures, it may be necessary to first establish whether the signature capturing procedure is reliable. In this sense, legal professionals may want to consult with both a forensic computer expert and handwriting expert in such cases. Additionally, it is advised that handwriting experts become more aware of electronic signature standards to ensure that the signatures they are examining have been sufficiently and securely captured.

4.12 SUMMARY

The Electronic Signature Act of 2000 made electronic signatures just as legally binding in transactions as traditional pen and ink signatures. Electronic signatures are now widely used internationally in all areas of commerce and business. There are challenges associated with electronic signatures concerning privacy and security, and while PINs and passwords have some advantages over handwritten signatures, biometric signatures provide information as to identity that PINs and passwords cannot provide. Digital and electronic signatures represent different "signatures." Digital signatures are cryptographic algorithms, while an electronic signature can be a scanned signature that is digitized, or it can be a handwritten signature that is captured on a digital tablet with a stylus, touch pad, or mouse. There are many different tablet types and electronic writing instrument devices, which increases variability problems in electronic handwriting. The digitization of signatures has helped in creating handwriting recognition technology and automated forensic handwriting analysis technology. Standards in the field have been developed to establish minimum security and quality measures in the implementation of electronic signatures.

Forensic Analysis of Electronic Signatures

The electronic capture of handwritten signatures presents novel opportunities and challenges in forensic signature analysis. Electronic signatures that capture dynamic movement allow for the analysis of temporal handwriting characteristics, characteristics not previously possible in the examination of traditional pen-and-paper signatures. The challenges that electronic signatures present to forensic examiners were reviewed previously by Franke (2007a) and LaVelle (2007).

With the increasing use of electronic signatures, document examiners need to develop methods of analysis in order to reliably conduct examinations of these new technology-based signatures. Research into temporal handwriting features presents a new level of forensic identification previously unknown in the analysis of pen-and-paper (or wet) signatures. While temporal features add a deeper, more significant layer of identification to handwriting, the devices used to record the measurements of the manuscript signature differ widely in technology. Temporal features such as the speed, pressure, and velocity are not available in all electronic signature cases—an inhibiting factor in forensic analysis. Some biometric systems incorporate computer-based dynamic analysis of signatures. However, experimental research needs to be conducted to establish whether these systems are adequate in capturing handwriting features that would allow forensic document examiners to recognize the possible false negatives caused by handwriting variables (i.e., health, disguise, and posture) or the possibility of false positives resulting from system attacks (forgery).

The low-resolution images recorded by many electronic signature systems make forensic analysis of digitized signatures either difficult or indeterminable. If these concerns are not addressed, the increasing use of electronic signatures may create significant forensic problems in signature identification cases, in that document examiners may not have the expertise or methods to examine electronic signatures; and forensic analysis may not be reliable because of the low-resolution graphic images that have limited or no temporal data.

With the onset of electronic signature technology, document examiners have little in the way of published methods or procedures in the analysis of electronic signatures, and limited experimental research has been published about this in the field of document examination. Some biometric handwriting research has been used to detect differences between genuine and forged signatures or healthy handwriting compared to handwriting that indicates the person has a movement disorder, but dynamic movement information is not always available in forensic casework. Although temporal information is sometimes accessible in examining dynamic signatures, document examiners have limited information about the technology and temporal features that can be analyzed.

5.1 PRACTICAL APPLICATION

From a forensic perspective, every signature that is signed may have forensic relevance. Signatures produced on point-of-sale devices for small dollar amounts hardly seem important. Forensic analysis of electronic signatures written on financial documents such as bank, loan, or insurance transactions seems more far more relevant, especially in terms of litigation. However, an electronic signature taken on a point-of-sale device at a retail store may place a suspect at the scene of a crime. Or a signature recorded on the e-signature capturing device of a courier service associated with a package containing illegal drugs also has forensic relevance. This means that poorly captured signatures or device problems compounds issues involved in forensic handwriting identification both in civil and criminal proceedings. Having access to the best evidence available in e-signature cases is important even in the most routine of transactions.

That cases involving handheld e-signature capture devices are forensically relevant is illustrated in the following internal affairs police case (Smith, 2009). Several motorists received traffic violations from a police officer, but subsequently complained that their signatures were forged on the citations. Police officers in the city used handheld PDAs for filling out citations and for capturing the signature of the traffic violator on the PDA's electronic display. A police witness reported that he saw the officer under investigation (his partner) forging the names of the traffic violators on the officer's PDA after the violator had driven away. Nearly 30 questioned traffic citation signatures that were captured on the PDA were sent to a forensic document examiner for analysis. The digitized signatures captured on the PDA were provided to the examiner in paper format, but not the digital files associated with the signature as no biometric data were captured. The examiner found that half of the questioned signatures exhibited significant dissimilarities to the signatures on the driver licenses for each of the traffic violators. Of those signatures, most of them showed high degrees of similarity suggesting that the same person wrote the signatures. Of the questioned signatures, four did not exhibit a sufficient degree of complexity in order to render an opinion.

Although limitations caused by the signing device in addition to not having biometric data precluded the examiner from giving stronger opinions, this was helped by the fact that the signatures were spurious. There was no attempt on the part of the forger to accurately imitate the spatial or movement dynamics of the genuine signatures, probably because the forger had no access to a signature at the time of writing since the violator had already driven away with their driver's license. As a result, the questioned signatures were little more than illegible loops and scrawls (Fig. 5.1). Because the forgeries were spurious (with little or no attempt to mimic the genuine writing format), it made it easier to determine that the signatures were not genuine. However, because the signatures were digitized, if there had been an attempt to mimic the real handwriting features, it would have been difficult to make a determination as to the authorship since there were no original signatures to examine and no biometric information had been captured with the e-signatures on the PDA device that would allow for an examination of

Fig. 5.1 Four examples of signatures signed on a police officer's PDA device.

the temporal characteristics of the signatures. While the examiner was able to offer opinions on most of the questioned signatures, there were several other limitations in this case which resulted in the examiner providing qualified or inconclusive opinions. Signing on a handheld PDA device creates awkward signing conditions. Further, electronically captured signatures were compared to manuscript signatures written with pen and ink that were later digitized. While both the questioned and known samples were digitized, the conditions in which they were signed were very different. This illustrates the limitations involved with e-signatures when no biometric information is available.

5.2 E-SIGNATURE SIGNING PROCESS AND STANDARDIZATION

There is not much question as to the acceptance of e-signatures so much as whether they are reliable. Defending an electronic signature in court can be more difficult than defending wet ink signatures. Establishing an original wet ink signature and determining its authorship is a well-defined process in forensic handwriting identification. The process in proving whether an e-signature is genuine or fraudulent is far less defined. Further, there is more involved in its forensic examination. If there is something questionable about the reliability of the data in an e-signature's capture, the expertise of a digital evidence specialist may be necessary in addition to that of a forensic handwriting expert.

In legally defending e-signatures, Silanis Technology, Inc. (2010) states that "if the process is clear to the signer, and organizations can prove that its customers knowingly consented to the terms and conditions of the agreement, the courts will enforce the electronic transaction" (p. 2). Silanis points out some minimum requirements in which litigators and experts should be aware when examining e-signatures: signatures are date and time stamped; signatures are unalterable without detection; data are secure and easily retrievable; and the e-signature process meets minimum state and federal compliance.

Standardization is a critical issue in electronic signing processes and technology. If manufacturers and users of the technology do not comply with the minimum standards established within the industry, the signature produced by this type of technology could be deemed unreliable. Even when manufacturers state that they meet the requirements established by the Electronic Signatures in Global and National Commerce Act (Federal Trade Commission, 2001) or the International Organization for Standardization (2005): ISO/IEC 27001:2005, these standards or minimum requirements for compliance apply to all forms of electronic signatures but may mean little to the handwriting expert examining a static or dynamic signature. From a practical standpoint, the level of awareness that the legal system, and, even, forensic examiners have regarding the minimum standards and procedures required for capturing and authenticating an electronic signature is questionable. This is a critical point, because in establishing procedures for handwriting examiners in evaluating these types of signatures, it may be necessary to first establish whether the signature capturing procedure is reliable. In some instances, it may be necessary for legal professionals to consult with both a digital evidence specialist and a document examiner.

Establishing inter-writer and intra-writer variability has always been an issue of concern in the field of forensic handwriting examination and was specifically mentioned as a problem area in forensic handwriting analysis in the National Research Council of the National Academies of Science Report (2009) on strengthening forensic science in the United States. With the onset of electronic signature technology, the issue of variability increases due to the numerous software, tablet, and stylus types currently on the market. Without an adequate understanding and knowledge of the associated software and hardware involved, the signature image provided to a handwriting examiner could be inadequate. This means that using standard methods and procedures in the forensic analysis of electronic signatures is necessary. A standard method would take into account the type of signature, software system, hardware devices, reliability and security of data, available handwriting features, and comparable comparison standards.

5.3 TECHNOLOGICAL CONSIDERATIONS

There are several points that forensic document examiners need to consider when analyzing an electronic signature. The technology involved in creating an e-signature needs to be evaluated before conducting an analysis of the handwriting characteristics. There is considerable variety in the methods used to capture electronic signatures, which brings into question issues concerning external factors in signature production (such as using a stylus or mouse to write the signature), the sampling rate and accuracy to record the signature (hertz), tablet quality, and transmission of data.

One of the issues associated with the capture of the measurements of a signature is how the document examiner obtains access to the computer file containing the electronic signature. When a person signs their signature on an electronic device, their actions are converted into measurements, as instructed by the software, and the data is then, in turn, translated into a series of digital data which is capable of being replicated on the screen (or printed onto paper) in the form of a graphic representation of the handwritten signature. The graphic representation of the signature is not the only data that the forensic document examiner should be reviewing. If the forensic document examiner is provided with a hard copy of the static signature image for examination, this may not be the best evidence that should be examined or presented to the court. Many of these signatures are captured at a low resolution with a pixelation effect replacing the smooth line quality of a handwritten signature. Sometimes the digital data comprising the signatures are affixed or incorporated into the document on a signature line in an unnatural way, or the signature's natural size may be significantly reduced—or both of these effects might occur. If the forensic document examiner receives a print-out of an electronic signature, such indications may show evidence that the signature was captured electronically. If these factors are present, the forensic document examiner should make inquiries about how the signature was produced and require a copy of the electronic signature file, because it is the digital data that must be examined, not only its representation. If the digital data exist, these need to be examined, because they provide the relevant information about the biometric properties of the purported signer, not the static image reproduced on paper.

Aside from examining the handwriting features that may have been recorded, some of the first steps in examining digital signature files is to inquire whether the file has been stored and processed in a way that allows for forensic signature analysis. Certain computer processing procedures are carried out in order to facilitate the feature extraction process. For example, different digital renditions of signatures, no matter how poor, may need to be moved, rescaled, and rotated to allow optimal comparison, thereby further cumulating the coarseness of pixelation (Afsar et al., 2005).

Packet loss, or the loss of digital data transmitted over the Internet, can occur in signature verification systems (Richiardi et al., 2004). There may have been distortion or loss of data during the transmission or processing of the data. During recording, ideally a signature is recorded at a constant sampling rate. However, the computer processor may miss sequences of samples. This implies that small parts of the signature may be missing purely due to the technology, and not because the writer was omitting an essential part of the signature.

A simple experiment using a commercially available electronic signature system on the Internet showed some of the problems that could occur when a signature is not accurately captured. The e-signature system that was used in the experiment is so convenient that a user can sign their signature directly onto the computer screen with a mouse. Because the system does not capture signatures biometrically, the signatures are digitized and only a digitized representation of the signature is available for examination. In a practical experiment with the software, subjects signed on a piece of paper on top of a digital tablet with an inking pen which was connected to a laptop computer. The e-signature software recorded the signature at the same time, so that the inking signature written on paper was simultaneously captured on the software. Capturing the signature simultaneously on paper and digitally allowed for a side-by-side examination to analyze the differences between the two signature types.

Obviously, the digitization of the signatures showed differences that were expected, especially in the shading of the ink trace. There was no gray scale used in the digitization of the signatures, and so parts of the signatures, especially in the feathered beginning and ending strokes, were translated as blunt strokes. Smooth air strokes, and lifts in the signatures also appeared cut-off or blunt when digitized. While these findings were expected when dealing with the black and white digitization of a signature where gray scale is not used, a few other details were

Fig. 5.2 Example of pen-and-paper signature (top) compared to electronic signature (bottom) showing data loss. The final stroke (arrow) of the ink signature was not recorded in the electronic signature.

found that were not expected. When the pressure was very heavy on a penstroke, the system probably could not capture the stroke and did not record it (Fig. 5.2). Sometimes, an ending stroke was converted into a hook that was not visible in the static ink trace, or at least not nearly as pronounced. Other observations showed strokes that were also not present in the static ink trace such as points that touched the boundary of the software recording box which were converted into short vertical lines at the edges of the signature.

While these details may not necessarily preclude a handwriting examiner from making an authorship opinion, especially if the signature is sufficiently complex, in some cases these details could lead to erroneous opinions or at least prevent an examiner from making a conclusive opinion as comparing digitized signatures captured on digital tablets to wet ink signatures may exhibit significant differences.

In an experiment comparing two comparable brand name tablet PCs, one tablet PC sensor provided less-reliable sampling rate information than the other, which affected the performance of the signature verification system used on the tablet PC for enrollment (Alonso-Fernandez et al., 2005). With respect to biometric systems in general, it has been commented that research work on evaluating the quality of biometric systems is limited (Alonso-Fernandez et al., 2011).

It is noteworthy that in a research study on the performance of automatic signature verification systems, the researchers ensured that the electronic data matched the hard copy data through visual inspection of the signatures "in order to verify that no errors occurred during acquisition" (Liwicki, 2012, p. 28). Additionally, it was mentioned that reliability of the acquisition device is important so that the "data contains no significant noise or gaps" (p. 28). In the study, an inking digital pen was used with a Wacom tablet and data was captured at a sampling rate of 200 Hz. In another signature verification system study, no preprocessing of the data was conducted because signatures were captured at 200 Hz on a Wacom tablet (Tariq et al., 2011). Capturing at a high sampling rate meant that the data did not require smoothing, normalizing, resampling, or resizing. If using tablets with low resolution, preprocessing would have been necessary. This was avoided due to "the fact that valuable data is lost while pre-processing the data" (p. 12). Besides the problems that can occur with preprocessing, acquisition can also affect certain specific handwriting features such as pressure: "while features related to the signature shape are not dependent on the data acquisition device, presence of dynamic features, such as pressure at the pen tip or pen tilt, depend on the hardware used" (p. 11). The limit or threshold of information recorded or maintained in a signature that allows for forensic analysis has not been clearly established in research; however, the above-mentioned studies used devices and a sampling rate consistent with other electronic handwriting research studies that provided reliable, captured data.

Preprocessing is a critical procedure as it may significantly alter handwriting features. In Zhang et al. (2009), preprocessing was considered a necessary procedure prior to feature extraction in a handwriting recognition study for pen-based devices. The preprocessing procedure involved six stages: (1) elimination of duplicate points; (2) connection of broken strokes in characters that should be connected in order that the system could recognize the writing; (3) elimination of handwriting hooks because they create "false" characteristics (these small movements at the beginning and endings of letters are short in length but cause "great change in perspective"; (4) smoothing to remove noise caused by erratic movements; (5) resampling to make the sample points equidistant ("they appear equidistant in time but not in space" so this variation is removed in order to keep the original trajectory); and (6) size normalization which removes "variation of different writing size" (p. 1256).

While these preprocessing steps are necessary for handwriting recognition, they would have the effect of turning the script more into a readable "font" while removing identifying characteristics necessary for forensic analysis. Resampling and possibly smoothing and elimination of duplicate points particularly affects the line quality features that are so important for analysis (Fig. 5.3). Such procedures render examination of line quality useless and can mask simulation characteristics. Connection of broken strokes, elimination of writing hooks, and size normalization would impact the fine detail that make up individualizing characteristics in handwriting that are relied upon for identification. Some handwriting systems have fewer or different preprocessing steps, but if the handwriting produced on a pen-based system, such as

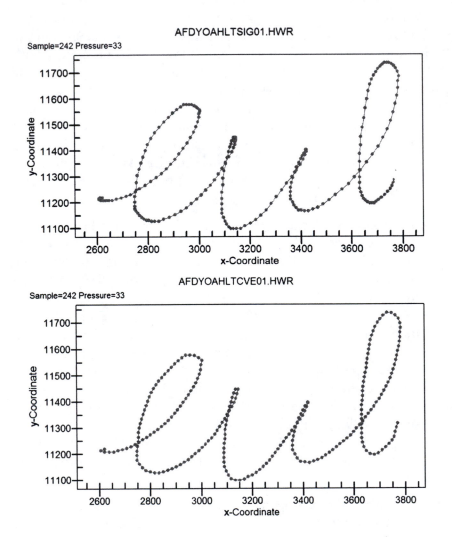

Fig. 5.3 Comparison of raw data (top) with resampled data showing equidistant sample points (bottom).

a PC tablet, were to come under forensic scrutiny, the examiner would need to know how the handwriting was preprocessed prior to beginning analysis of the handwriting features.

The analysis of electronic signatures involves an understanding of not only the software but also the hardware used to acquire the signature, including the way the purported signer may have interacted with the hardware. Aside from the variables associated with tablets, significant changes in temporal and spatial dimensions occur when signatures are written with digital writing implements in comparison to signatures written with ink and paper. These differences are caused both by the writing device and the writer's response to the writing device. Hardware factors such as the enlarged tip of a digital writing pen and the lack of friction on a digital tablet can cause changes to a writer's natural signature. The size of the writing tablet box or pad and other conditions associated with electronic signature capturing devices can have a varying effect on the way people respond to the device. Some web-based software programs instruct the signer to use a mouse or the fingertip while signing their signature into a box on a computer screen or digital display. Other devices have no visual feedback, delayed visual feedback, or poor resolution when signing on a signature pad. Some devices provide instructions to write within the parameters of a box, or require that the signature be captured within a certain time frame (or both). Frustration with rejected signatures and responding to annoying instructions may cause some people to alter their natural signature in order to fit within the box and within specified time limits. Some devices are handheld, which creates another factor pertaining to awkward posture while signing on a device.

Understanding the software and system used to capture the handwriting is critical in the examination. Some systems do not capture biometric data at all, while other systems capture varying degrees of biometric data. Some systems may only record a few measurements, while others may record the measurements of several handwriting features that would allow for a comprehensive forensic analysis of temporal and form-based elements.

In reviewing a few of the systems that are offered in the marketplace, it is evident that there is little consistency with respect to the way a signature is recorded. Topaz Systems, Inc. (2012) recommends software and hardware guidelines for the recording of a signature. Part of their signature recording process includes binding the signature to the document using a secure hash "which forms a direct cryptographic relationship between the signature and a single document or aggregated data message, and security data" (Topaz Systems, Inc., 2012). Topaz also records biometric signature measurements in some of its software products.

SOFTPRO GmbH (2012) software examines both static and dynamic information from signatures including location, pressure, and time signals. WonderNet's Penflow system requires users to enroll into the database by providing a total of six signatures, three of which are for training purposes. Once a user is enrolled into the system, the system continues to collect signatures and increases the size of the database of the measurements that are recorded. Penflow also includes additional security features such as a hash in order to invalidate the signature if the document is altered. Instead of writing a manuscript signature, the Biometric Signature ID (2012) software instructs users to sign into the system drawing a password with a mouse. The measurements that are recorded and analyzed include speed, direction, length, height, width, angle, and number of strokes.

Cyber-SIGN (Witswell Consulting & Services, 2009) affixes biometric signatures into portable document format (PDF) documents with the intention that the document and its associated signature cannot be altered without changes being detected. This is an example of a system where affixing the signature into the document is an important process in the act of "signing." Signature authentication and verification is achieved through Cyber-SIGN's signature verification algorithm, which examines changes in speed, shape, pressure, strokes, and air strokes.

DocuSign, Inc. (2012) includes affixing the signature measurements and other security features, but does not record a signature in a way that is a graphic representation of the handwritten signature. The user types in his or her name and can select a cursive-type font style in order to make the name look like a signature when it is affixed or logically associated with the document.

Some biometric-based handwriting systems perform automatic computerized signature analysis and verification. These types of systems are used for obtaining access or entry and are sometimes used instead of fingerprint, iris, or facial scans, because signatures cannot be replicated and are more user-friendly. However, there may be limitations in automatic signature verification with respect to system attacks (forgeries), handwriting variation, and data transmission loss.

There has been considerable research on the use of biometric signatures for identification and verification (Jain et al., 2002; Kholmatov & Yanikoglu, 2005). This research has yielded varied results. Some studies have shown that signature verification systems may have weaknesses that allow for successful forgery attacks (Ballard et al., 2006; Lopresti & Raim, 2005). A comparison of online and offline signature verification system methods showed that the performance between the two approaches differed little, which is surprising considering how much temporal information can be extracted from dynamic data (Rigoll & Kosmala, 1998).

A competition between automatic signature verification systems and forensic document examiners compared their performance (Liwicki et al., 2010). In the competition, disguised signatures were included in the sample set to test how automated systems performed with a difficult task. Performance varied across the seven systems used in the study. Averaging the scores of the systems for the number of signatures that were forged but accepted as genuine by the systems (false acceptance rate, FAR) was 23.4. The number of signatures that were genuine but rejected by the systems (false rejection rate, FRR) was 71.4. It was noted, however, that when retesting without the disguised signatures, system performance dramatically improved. By comparison, the forensic handwriting experts tested on the same data had 7.2% misleading opinions. Another study reports that that the "equal error rate of available online signature verification systems lies between 1 to 10%" (Tariq et al., 2011).

5.4 EVALUATING STATIC AND DYNAMIC HANDWRITING FEATURES

The forensic examination of electronic signatures is primarily concerned with identification and verification questions; for example, did the purported signer sign the electronic signature or not? This question necessarily involves examining the signature for signs of simulation, or what is popularly referred to as forgery, as well as other indicators that may involve variables that affect the natural state of the signature. Because this section concerns handwriting and signature feature analysis and its differentiation between natural writing and forged or simulated handwriting, it is necessary to diverge from electronic signatures and discuss the dynamic movement of naturally written signatures and their simulations.

The signature is one of the most practiced motor movements performed in one's lifetime, and certainly the most practiced handwriting movement. The writer performs the sequenced movements of the signature typically in a fast and fluent motion, sometimes connecting different elements of the signature into one fluid movement. The signature is normally written quickly, and the movement of the signature is so frequently rehearsed by the brain, nervous system, and muscles that it has become automatic. Therefore, it is not unusual for the signer to begin the movement in the air before the tip of the pen has hit the surface of the paper.

Some of the features associated with highly automatic signatures involve flying starts and feathered endings because the pen is already moving in the air to begin the well-practiced movements. This process can be likened to a spring-loaded movement, where the hand is moving into action before the pen hits the paper.

Fast fluid movements are associated with natural signatures. These fluid movements create the smooth lines in long curves and contribute greatly to the harmonious flow of the signature. Even transitions can have a fluid movement. Movement is also associated with a repetitious pressure pattern where the upstrokes of the curves have a lighter pressure while the downstrokes have a heavier pressure.

While these movements are fluent, they are not perfectly repetitive. The speed involved with a fast and fluent signature is also responsible for the range of variation present in one's collection of natural signatures. Typically, the faster and looser the writing, the greater the range of variation while slower, more precise writings will naturally have a lesser degree of natural variation between signatures. Fluency and speed increases at the cost of precision, while increased precision and attention to detail can diminish speed and natural fluency. When a person does not have a highly automatic signature, due to lack of graphic maturity or other complications, the signature will tend to have a slower, less automatic, and far less practiced or rehearsed movement pattern.

Signature simulation involves the imitation of a natural or genuine signature movement. This is also popularly referred to as forgery. There are certain types of forgeries referred to as simple or spurious forgeries where the forger merely signs the name of the victim, paying little or no attention to the actual form or style of the signature. Freehand simulations, however, are more complex and involve copying the signature form and style. In order to copy the signature, the forger must have access to one or more models of the signature and may have had the opportunity to practice signing the signature once or twice or over several years. When the forger pays attention to the form of the signature, because the movement has not become automatic, the forger's movement may or may not accurately capture the genuine signature, but in the process, the forger's movements are slow and constrained while copying the signature. As a result, the dynamic, fluent movement of the signature is not imitated accurately, frequently resulting in writing line quality that is tremulous, slow, and deliberate. There may be stops or breaks in the line, hesitations, uncharacteristic lifts, and slow starts and endings. The pressure may have an unusual pattern or lack of normal pressure dynamics.

The forger may have had long experience in practicing the signature and be a skilled writer, which sometimes happens in cases where children may have been practicing their parent's signature for years, or spouses are used to signing for each other taking pride in the meticulous way in which they have imitated their spouse's signature. How frequently have we heard a husband say that his wife can imitate his signature so well that he can't tell the difference between his signature and her imitation? In these instances, the forger may capture not only the form but also some of the dynamism of natural writing movement. However, in instances where a forger may not be skilled or well-practiced, the forger, in trying to imitate the fast movement, or just writing in a fast or careless manner, may capture some of the fluent movement dynamics while sacrificing the form details of the signature.

Retraced signatures involve the nearly exact replication of a signature model. This can be achieved by tracing over the genuine signature in such a way where an indentation or image of the signature is copied onto a surface under the signature model. This can also be achieved in using transmitted light (such as a lightbox) so that the image of the signature is seen through another sheet of paper and a tracing can be created. In these types of forgeries, the form details of the signature are replicated fairly accurately, but the line quality is typically very poor. The line quality is slow, drawn, hesitant, and slightly tremulous. There

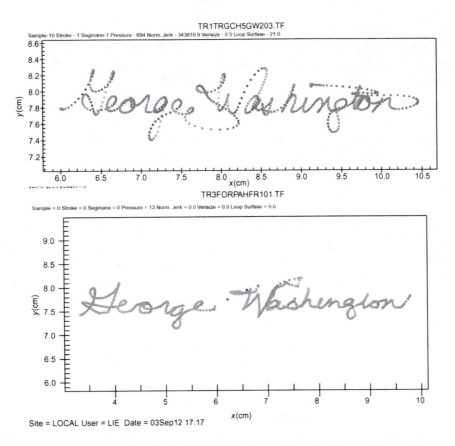

TR1TRGCH5GW203.TF

Sample-10 Stroke - 1 Segmane-1 Pressure - 694 Norm. Jerk - 343819.9 Verisize - 0.3 Loop Surfase - 21.0

TR3FORPAHFR101.TF

Sample = 0 Stroke = 0 Segmane = 0 Pressure = 13 Norm. Jerk = 0.0 Verisize = 0.0 Loop Surfase = 0.0

Site = LOCAL User = LIE Date = 03Sep12 17:17

Fig. 5.4 Handwriting samples captured on the MovAlyzeR showing sampling points. The top writing sample is natural writing that shows longer distances between the sample points (indicating faster writing). The bottom writing sample is a simulation with very little space (or speed) between the sample points.

may be unusual breaks which are sometimes corrected with patches. Blunt stops may occur in the middle of what should be smooth movements, and the beginning and ending strokes are slow and blunt as well (see Fig. 5.4).

In the literature of forensic document examiners, poor line quality characteristics have been classically associated with simulated movement (Conway, 1959; Harrison, 1958; Hilton, 1993; Huber & Headrick, 1999; Osborn, 1929). The ASTM Standard Guide for Examination of Handwritten Items (2007) specifically lists certain characteristics that examiners should take special note of if they are present: "lifts, stops and hesitations of the writing instrument; patching and retouching;

slow, drawn quality of the line; unnatural tremor; and guide lines of various forms should be evaluated when present" (p. 3).

With the advent of digital tablets and software that captures online handwriting electronically, research has confirmed some of the characteristics that were observed in the static ink pen trace. Handwriting examination observations have been validated through handwriting movement research and technology, as there were certain observed characteristics that were based on rough estimates of the static trace. For example, evaluating the speed in writing from the static ink trace can yield some estimates, especially in comparing it relative to other samples. If one sample exhibits natural movements with fluency and tapering end strokes and this is compared to another sample that exhibits stops, hesitations, and unnatural breaks, such a comparison will undoubtedly lead the examiner to make the prediction that the former signature is the one that is written more rapidly.

With electronic handwriting technology, these estimates that forensic document examiners predict (based on static features in the handwriting) can be confirmed and validated. One of the first studies to examine the kinematic movement differences between natural and simulated handwriting movement confirmed what was popularly recognized by forensic handwriting experts: simulations are produced slowly and dysfluently (Van Gemmert & Van Galen, 1996). In comparing the results of natural handwriting to experimental simulations, "results showed a trend towards prolonged reaction times, significantly increased movement times, [and] significantly more dysfluencies" (p. 459). Other research into handwriting examiner skill has found that handwriting examiners were accurate in their speed estimates when comparing handwriting samples written at different speeds (Will, 2012). Capturing at high hertz rates (200 Hz/s yields 200 samples per second), the speed profile can be easily determined electronically by examining the length of space between each sample point (Fig. 5.4). The more space between the sample points, the faster the writing speed. By comparison, the second sample in Fig. 5.4 shows how there is little to no space between the sample points in a simulated handwriting.

Experimental research into the temporal characteristics of handwriting movement has produced a profile of the movement characteristics of a natural signature and of a simulated signature. This research has created a new layer for analysis of handwriting characteristics, based upon the temporal aspects of the signature rather than its form-based static features. Sophisticated handwriting capturing software has the ability to determine far more from stroke movement than just its duration.

Duration measures the length of time of a stroke or a handwritten movement such as a signature. Other dynamic features that are even more identifying characteristics as to the movement pattern of a signer involve velocity and acceleration. Velocity, with respect to handwriting, is the speed and direction of the stroke while acceleration involves the change of velocity in a handwriting pattern (Fig. 5.5). The electronics

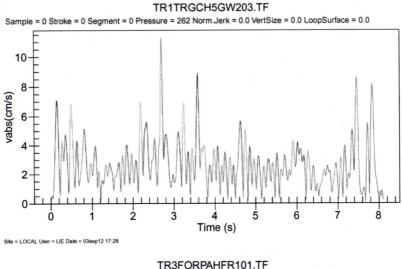

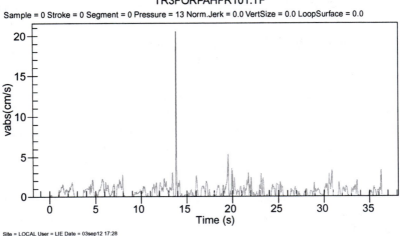

Fig. 5.5 Absolute velocity charted for natural writing (top) and its simulation (bottom). Note that the natural writing took 8 s to write while the bottom sample took over 35 s to produce.

inside some digital pens that were initially invented for graphic designers can measure pressure patterns in handwriting. Pressure patterns are caused by a combination of force and time and rather than making rough estimates about the amount of pressure used in a static stroke trace, pressure and its pattern can now be defined quantitatively using handwriting movement capture (Fig. 5.6). While the horizontal and vertical dimensions of writing are referred to as the x- and y-axis, pressure is referred to as the z-axis.

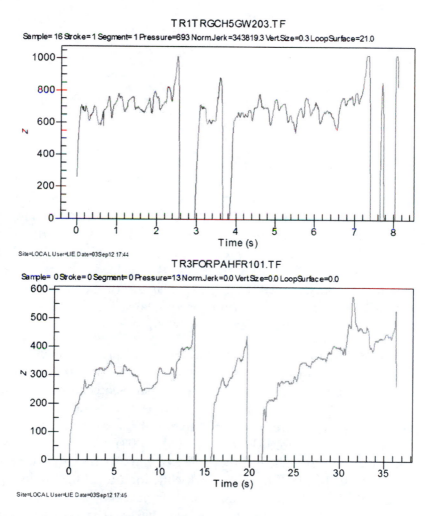

Fig. 5.6 Axial pressure (z-axis) charted for a natural writing (top) and its simulation (bottom). The natural writing has a much higher pressure score than its simulation.

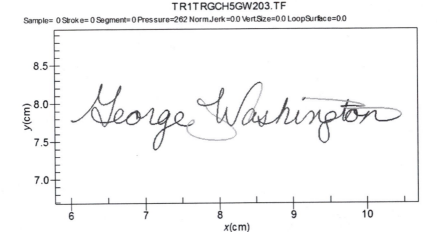

TR1TRGCH5GW203.TF

Sample= 0 Stroke= 0 Segment= 0 Pressure=262 Norm.Jerk=0.0 VertSize=0.0 LoopSurface=0.0

Site=LOCAL User=UE Date=03Sep12 18:27

Fig. 5.7 Example of air stroke movements in natural writing. The red lines show the air strokes and the blue lines show the pen-downstrokes. (For interpretation of the references to color in this figure legend, the reader is referred to the web version of this book.)

Electronic capture of signatures allows for the quantitative analysis and comparison of natural handwriting movement to simulation. Studies that compare these areas have shown that simulated handwriting movement has longer duration times as well as decreased velocity and acceleration (Sita & Rogers, 1999; Thomassen & Van Galen, 1997; Van Gemmert & Van Galen, 1996). The velocity spectrum was compared and analyzed in studies on simulated writing and showed a significantly weaker force spectrum for simulated writing (Harralson et al., 2008; Van Gemmert & Van Galen, 1996).

Air strokes are another unique identifier for examining fluency and speed in writing. Air strokes can be captured and analyzed because movement is recorded even when the digital pen is a centimeter above the tablet surface. One study found that it was easy to capture the air stroke movements of natural writers because the strokes in the air did not stray far from the tablet (Harralson et al., 2008). However, observation of forger behavior showed that some of the experimental subjects tended to lift the pen far from the tablet while looking at the model signature and deciding on how to execute their next movement. In order to capture the recording, the forgers were asked to keep their pens closer to the surface of the tablet (Fig. 5.7).

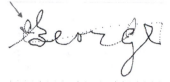

Fig. 5.8 Example of restarting (arrow) beginning the stroke in a simulation.

Fig. 5.9 Example of correcting part of a signature during simulation. The air stroke shows the path of the pen as the writer goes back to the initial letter to correct (arrow) a stroke.

Experimental research has captured recordings of subjects restarting the movement at the beginning of the simulated signature (Fig. 5.8) where the forger stopped at the beginning of the movement, creating a dot (Harralson et al., 2008). The forger lifted the pen and restarted again unsure at first how to imitate the model of the writing. Another forger in the same experiment corrected a part of the signature by going back to the beginning of the signature and adding a stroke in order to correct part of the initial letter's form (Fig. 5.9). An air stroke recording shows the movement of the writer moving back across the signature in order to make the correction.

Historically, most forensic handwriting examination casework has involved static analysis of ink signatures. The features examined for signatures committed to a piece of paper differ from biometric methods of signature capture, yet information obtained from dynamic features could help facilitate or validate static observations. For example, characteristics typical of forgery include blunt initial and terminal strokes and slowly drawn line quality (ASTM, 2007). These can be recorded, measured, and recovered through biometric methods. Pen speed can be precisely measured but only estimated when analyzing pen-and-paper signatures. Dynamic methods not only improve upon, but are superior to, analysis of static signature characteristics, because of the temporal information that can be recorded and quantified.

Review of handwriting feature extraction studies can be used as a starting point in establishing what can be reliably analyzed from dynamic signature analysis. From a practical perspective, however, some of the dynamic electronic signatures encountered in document examination cases are static images rather than the original digital data, which means that the best evidence available is not always provided to the forensic document examiner.

Some of the well-known features that can be analyzed via online methods include duration, stroke sequence, velocity, acceleration, pressure, and other factors. While there are many handwriting features that can be utilized in biometric systems, not all features are used. Nor are even the most reliable and consistent features used in biometric handwriting systems (Lei & Govindaraju, 2005). While sophisticated systems could be produced, and some are available, cost and convenience factors prohibit their widespread use.

There have been several experimental studies on recovering dynamic and temporal information from static handwriting (Boccignone et al., 1993; Cha et al., 2004; Doermann & Rosenfeld, 1995; Franke & Grube, 1998; Schirripa Spagnolo, 2005; Senatore et al., 2011). The techniques and information from these studies may be helpful in understanding the features that can be extracted from static signatures as well as how to interpret results. Online handwriting feature extraction is being used as a tool in forensic handwriting research (Halder-Sinn & Funsch, 1998; Harralson et al., 2008; Longstaff & Heath, 2000; Phillips et al., 2000; Sita & Rogers, 1999; Thomassen & Van Galen, 1997; Van Galen & Van Gemmert, 1996; Van Gemmert & Van Galen, 1996). Review of these studies establishes what can be successfully analyzed from online signature analysis. Most of the studies examine dynamic, online recordings. From a practical perspective, many electronic signatures encountered in document examination cases are digitized images rather than recordings, so studies on how temporal data can be extracted from static images are helpful.

Scheidat et al. (2007) found that there were problems in relying on class characteristics in online handwriting verification, especially when users wrote a handwritten PIN number. An experiment comparing signatures, numerals, and sentences found that the complexity involved with signatures was more secure biometrically than writing numeral-based PIN numbers and sentences. However, the researchers found that a system was significantly more secure when relying on more than one handwriting-based strategy; security was increased when fusing a signature, sentence, and/or handwritten PIN number.

Evaluation of online and offline signature research can help define the minimum standard that signature capturing devices need to implement in order that signatures can be analyzed, in a reliable way, forensically. This is particularly important since the data that can be recovered from the analysis of online data exceeds the data that can be analyzed utilizing offline approaches but only if the correct type of online data is captured.

In examining the reliability of data captured by biometric verification systems, it was found that some measurements provide more consistent and discriminating data than others (Lei & Govindaraju, 2005). While it is generally accepted that handwriting factors such as velocity, acceleration, and pressure are more difficult to forge, we may not know if they are reliable features. These researchers remark that there are multiple features available when developing biometric handwriting systems, and more features are being invented, so it is important to know which features are the most reliable when performing signature analysis. Since there are usually a limited number of handwriting exemplars available for comparison, it is even more critical that the handwriting features are consistent and reliable. In their study (Ibid.), 22 features were evaluated for consistency. An analysis of some of the results showed that azimuth (direction of the projection of the pen onto the writing plane) and altitude (steepness or height of the pen) had high standard deviations which reduce their discriminatory value. Curvature-ellipse (curve radius), torque (rotational force), and center of mass may be useful for detecting random forgeries but are not so useful for detecting skilled forgeries. Although pressure is frequently discussed as a valuable feature for detecting forgeries, it was found that the feature was not very consistent within natural writing. As a result, large variation in pressure between samples is not a good indicator of forgery, but a similar pressure pattern is suggestive of genuine writing. The features that showed consistency and reliability included the speed of the x- and y-coordinates, the x- and y-coordinate sequence, and the angle with the x-axis.

Another study examined local and global features for online systems to determine which had the most efficient and most discriminating power for signature verification (Richiardi et al., 2005). Local features are based on a single data point in the signature while global features extract a feature based on the signature as an entire unit. Out of 46 global features, some of the features that showed the strongest discriminatory characteristics included pressure measurements which "is in line with many reported results in the literature that pressure is an important distinguishing feature between signers" (p. 3). Other global features included velocity measurements and pen-down samples. Some of the most significant local features included local pressure measures, vertical and horizontal position, pen azimuth, pen elevation, velocity measures, acceleration measures, and radius of curvature.

In another study that evaluated strong and weak features in an intelligent, online signature verification system (Tariq et al., 2011), the researchers classified more than 100 features and, using analysis of each feature's standard deviations, they narrowed down the number of features used in the study. Features with stronger results included total time, various velocity and acceleration measurements, average pressure, length, and pen-down time.

In selecting robust online features, Liwicki (2012) listed several measurements that included horizontal and vertical positions, pressure, acceleration measures, pen azimuth, and pen elevation. Offline features are based on gray-scale values and pixels and may seem to have little in common with handwriting characteristics that document examiners would recognize. However, pixel gradients, black–white transitions, and average gray value of pixels is digital language that expresses line quality and ink-trace features that are an important component in forensic handwriting examination analysis. These types of features are typically evaluated by a handwriting expert with a microscope and are considered line quality characteristics.

It has been pointed out, though, that the best features used in evaluating electronic signatures are dependent upon the specific handwriting as certain features may be more identifying for one person's handwriting, but not for another's (Liwicki, 2012; Tariq et al., 2011).

5.5 FORGERY AND SYSTEM ATTACKS

From a practical perspective, attempting forgery on an electronic signature device presents some challenges to the handwriting task for the forger just as it does to the genuine, natural signer. Frequently, such a device is employed at a point-of-sale type of transaction, or, for example, when signing at a bank in the presence of a witness. There are "over-the-shoulder" attacks: this term refers to a potential forger watching another person sign a signature on an electronic device and then attempting to simulate the signature based on what has been observed. A study evaluating a biometric signature system showed that it performed well against over-the-shoulder attacks (Alpcan et al., 2008).

Naturally, over-the-shoulder attacks are not likely to produce very effective forgeries as the forger typically has little time to watch the signer produce their signature, does not have a model signature to copy readily available, has to rely on his or her memory, and may not have the opportunity to practice the signature. One advantage to the forger, however, is that he or she may be able to watch the movement dynamics of the signer rather than attempting to copy from the static trace model of the signature. It is the movement dynamics that make biometric signatures more secure, so increased study into these types of attacks could prove enlightening, especially in comparison to pen-and-paper forgery methods.

A more traditional forging method involves what is referred to as freehand simulation. In this type of forgery, the forger has access to a copy of the signature and practices the model of the signature in order to simulate it. Freehand simulation accuracy is dependent upon the skill of the writer and it has been demonstrated in forensic handwriting examiner proficiency testing that practiced and skilled forgeries increase error and inconclusive rates in expert opinions (Dewhurst et al., 2008).

If the forger has access to an electronic signature and a digital tablet, practice would be possible. This could happen especially with spouses signing each other's names (with or without the intent to defraud). It has been repeatedly demonstrated that forgers perform better in replicating the static features of the signature than they do in replicating the dynamic features such as speed. Because forgery is not a natural skill that has been programmed into the writer's neuro-motor memory, the forgery task increases difficulty and it takes more time to imitate the signature's static features. In order to imitate the writer's natural movement dynamics, the forger would lose accuracy in the signature's static features. This trade-off has frequently been analyzed in assessing forgery as these dynamic features are also present in static analysis of signatures. In examining biometric signatures, it is even easier to quantify the amount of time it takes to sign an authentic signature and compare it to a questioned signature. In this sense, biometric signatures are superior to static signatures in exhibiting the signature's underlying movement features.

While systems on the market have boasted that biometric signatures are forgery-proof, a fool proof system is dependent on many factors. It is true that biometric signature analysis based on the movement dynamics of the signature is superior to analysis of static features alone. However, some systems do not always capture enough movement features or the most reliable features. Additionally, there are other factors that could confound the analysis of genuine versus forged signatures. If a signature has low complexity, for example, it is easier to imitate both the static and dynamic features of the signature. If a signature is both simple and highly variable, this could also complicate problems, since such signatures are easier to imitate. A high degree of variation could lead to a false rejection by the system. To avoid this, the signer may adopt a more consistent signature pattern in order to obtain system access. While the system is involved in "training" the signer to write more consistently, this could lead to an overly regular pattern which could have the unintentional effect of making it easier for the forger to imitate more successfully.

In the digital world, forgers are not limited to "over-the-shoulder" freehand simulations. Tracing can be accomplished, perhaps more effectively, through digitization than through conventional pen-and-paper methods. A signature can be traced onto a tablet and captured. The forger can then manipulate the data of the captured signature to create a digitized image that resembles fluid movement dynamics typical of genuine signatures (Fig. 5.10). This is accomplished through filtering the data using constant distancing of the sample points (equidistant sample points). Without reliable biometric data to assess the dynamic features, a traced signature captured electronically is less difficult to detect than a traced signature written with pen on paper. The biometric data needs to capture the writing using constant frequency of the sampling points because that is how speed measures are determined in the handwriting strokes. Detection of certain traced forgeries can only be determined through analysis of the captured data, not via analysis of the handwriting image.

5.6 LIMITATIONS

In comparison to traditional pen-and-paper signatures, some electronic signature capture methods alter the dynamic movement of handwriting. These differences occur at the beginning of the process (when the purported signer is using the equipment such as a stylus or tablet), as

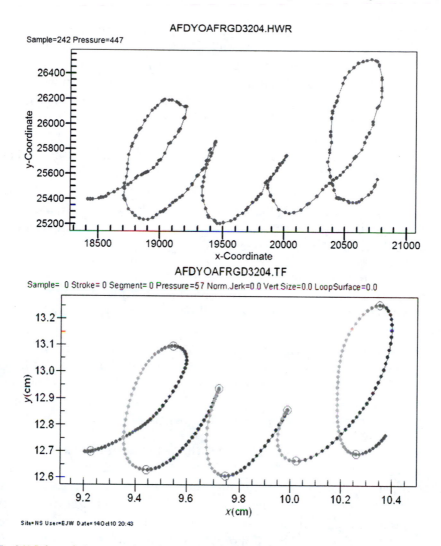

Fig. 5.10 *Before and after images of traced (unfiltered) and digitally manipulated (filtered) handwriting strokes.*

well as arising from the method in which the measurements of the signature are recorded and processed in accordance with the instructions set out in the software. A proper analysis of the signature not only must examine the printed version of the signature measurements but should include the digital data and software that enables measurements such as speed and pressure to be recorded.

One of the potential problems that can occur in the analysis of electronic signatures involves the comparison of an electronically captured signature with traditional pen-and-paper signatures. First, writing with a stylus on a tablet in a box or onto a computer screen is a different writing environment from writing on paper with a pen. Experimental studies have shown significant differences in the way a person writes his or her signature on e-signature capture devices compared with writing an ink signature on paper. For example, handwriting measurements or characteristics that changed between electronic signing and traditional signing included the writing velocity and size (Harralson et al., 2011). Additionally, a detailed analysis of the form characteristics between the two conditions showed differences. The differences were significant, in that the form details that changed between the signature conditions could be attributed to either an altered writing environment or could be mistakenly attributed to the effect of forgery (Fig. 5.11).

Results from the Harralson et al. (2011) study also showed that when writers attempt to sign legibly on signature capture devices with altered visual feedback (a box on a computer screen), writing time tends to increase. Using a digital tablet pen also tends to cause a change in writing size, especially in the horizontal dimension. In examining individual subject results, it was observed that some subjects approach the awkwardness of signing with a mouse by simplifying their signature. Additionally, writers make adjustments to their signature in order to adapt to device constraints (e.g., writing inside a box).

Interestingly, the study showed that the writer with the least complex signature showed very little difference across the three conditions (ink, digital pen, and mouse). This is in contrast to another subject with a highly complex and fluent signature, who showed significant differences across the three conditions. It was also observed that some subjects who have complex signatures had a more difficult time writing with the digital pen and mouse, and that a few made adjustments to their signature by simplifying the signatures. It was found that, with longer and more complex signatures, some subjects dealt with running out of space in the signing box by compressing their signature or simplifying it. In signing with the mouse, a few subjects simplified it to the point that it was no longer the same signature as their ink signature (Fig. 5.12).

In handwriting, complexity refers to a theory that evaluates the number of turning points and intersection points to derive an estimate as to whether the signature has enough graphic features with which to form an opinion (Found & Rogers, 1998). Three levels of complexity

DIGDIGJLPSG303.TF

Sample= 0 Stroke= 0 Segment=0 Pressure=17 Norm.Jerk=0.0 VertSize=0.0 LoopSurface=0.0

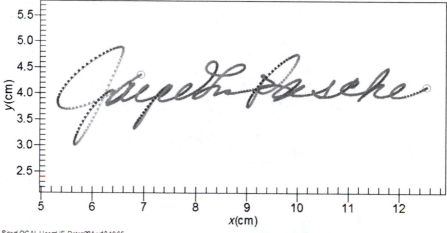

Site=LOCAL User=LIE Date=28Apr12 10:06

DIGDIGJLPSG401.TF

Sample= 0 Stroke= 0 Segment= 0 Pressure=3 Norm.Jerk =0.0 VertSize=0.0 LoopSurface=0.0

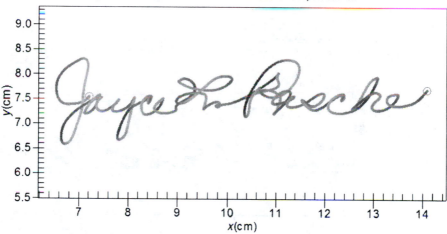

Site=LOCAL User=LIE Date=28Apr12 09:57

Fig. 5.11 Signature written with ink on paper (top) compared to signature written with digital pen on tablet with visual feedback on computer screen (bottom). Some of the fine detail in the signature is lost in the second signature (e.g., point on top of the "s" and complex movements in lowercase "c").

were formulated. Level 1 has several intersections and turning points in the signature which allow for conclusive opinions as to authorship. Level 2 complexity has a moderate level of complexity which allows for qualified authorship opinions while Level 1 complexity does not have sufficient complexity features and allows only for inconclusive

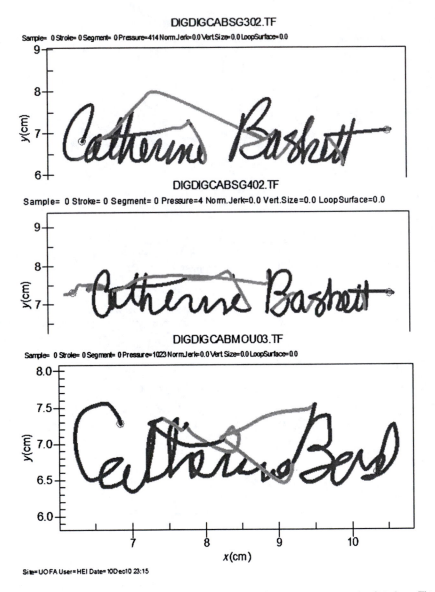

Fig. 5.12 *The top signature is written with an ink pen on paper. Second signature is written with a digital pen. Third signature is written with a mouse. The writer adjusts the length of the signature in the second and third conditions due to space constraint when trying to write inside a box on a computer screen.*

authorship opinions. The findings in the electronic signature study are important to analyze with respect to complexity, because if a signer is adapting the signature to device constraints by reducing its complexity, this can impact the ability of a forensic handwriting expert to form an opinion about its authorship. For example, one subject in the study had a Level 1 complex signature allowing for conclusive authorship opinions. In adapting to the constraints in signing with a mouse, the subject simplified her signature to the point where it bordered on a Level 3 complex signature, which only allows for an inconclusive opinion as to authorship (Fig. 5.13).

A practical experiment compared signatures across four signing conditions: (1) signing with ink pen on paper; (2) signing on a Topaz signature tablet using a stylus and "digital ink" visual feedback on the display; (3) signing on a pressure-sensitive digital tablet using a stylus and no visual feedback on the display; and (4) signing on the same pressure-sensitive digital tablet using a fingertip and no visual feedback on the display. The eight subjects in the experiment knew how to write in cursive and had no significant health problems that would seriously impair their handwriting. The writing samples were all taken at the same time period, so as to limit the variation that can occur on different days. Two different Topaz signature tablets were used to capture the three different e-signature conditions; one tablet was pressure-sensitive while the other had a digital ink display. The signatures were captured and saved using Topaz SigPlus software. All the subjects wrote on and observed the digital tablets in front of them; they did not watch the recording of the signature on a computer screen.

In analyzing the signatures, Topaz SigCompare software was used for visual comparison of signatures. The software allows for a comparison of two electronic signatures at a time and is designed for bank tellers, cashiers, and others who encounter signatures in daily transactions and need a quick and efficient signature comparison tool. The instructions on the comparison screen state that "for two signatures to match, the shape and shading must both be similar" (Topaz Systems, Inc., 2004). Using Topaz's trademarked "Dynamic Shading" technique based on the velocity of the signature, the software includes six comparison adjustments that can be selected. The default is 0 and shows both signatures in their raw digitized format. The other levels show the signature's velocity profiles using thick lines to indicate slower movement and thin lines to indicate fast movement. Using these graphic velocity profiles, one can examine the shaded pattern within the signature to determine if the patterns between the two signatures are similar as well as examine the signatures for the presence of natural movement. Natural movement, as established in the kinematic handwriting literature, indicates that short, narrow curves take a longer time to produce

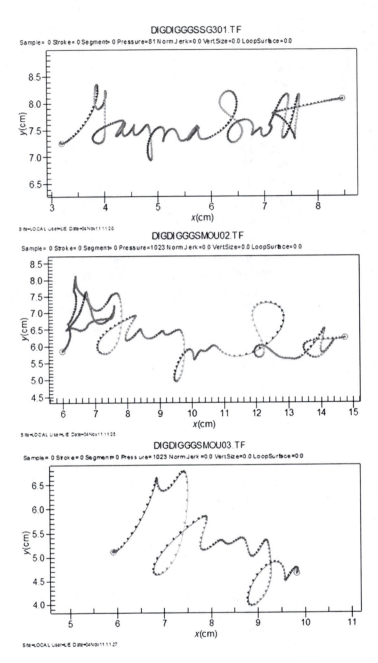

Fig. 5.13 Top signature is written with ink on paper. Second signature is the writer's second attempt to sign with a mouse. By the third attempt, the writer simplified her signature to make signing with the mouse easier.

while long, wide curves take a shorter time to produce. As a result, a slow simulation would exhibit a Topaz shading profile of thick lines throughout the signature without any or very little natural velocity pattern present.

A comparison of the four signatures showed ways that the subjects approached signatures in these different e-signature writing conditions. The ability to see one's signature while writing it either with a pen on paper or through digital ink feedback on a display allows the writer more flexibility and freedom to lift the pen for breaks. The signatures produced while signing on the tablet with no visual feedback (both stylus and fingertip) showed fewer breaks in the writing even between the first and last name. Sometimes details such as lowercase "i" dots were missing from signatures when there was no visual feedback. This is not a surprising finding because going back to dot an "i" on a signature that is not visible is not very practical. In comparison, the dot on the "i" was placed when signers wrote on the display tablet with visual feedback.

In some instances, even though a pressure-sensitive tablet was used for the fingertip condition, the software did not always fully capture the fingertip pressure. Some subjects stated that their fingertip got stuck on the pressure-sensitive tablet, which would have affected the recording of the signature. Signing with one's fingertip shows some similarities to signing with a mouse in that the signatures are awkward and appear too large for the space in which they are written. There is an emphasis on horizontal expansion and lack of coordination in signatures signed with the finger. The horizontal expansion is caused by the broad tip of the finger, which is not capable of making narrow curves, and small, delicate movements. Loss of fine detail was also found in signatures written with a stylus (Fig. 5.14).

Experimental research into the properties of signatures that are written in varying e-signature environments helps forensic examiners to characterize these different conditions, especially when comparing to other signatures that were not written in a similar electronic environment. When analyzing questioned e-signatures, the examiner can use this experimental research to determine if such differences are characteristic of device signing conditions or if they are the product of some other process such as simulation. Another alternative is that the variability caused by certain e-signature conditions may warrant

Fig. 5.14 Examples of three electronic signatures written with different writing implements: first signature written on digital ink pad with stylus; second signature written on digital tablet with no visual feedback using stylus; and third signature written on a pressure-sensitive pad with finger. Due to no visual feedback, the second signature is much more connected than the first signature. The problems with the third signature were partially caused by the finger sticking to the pad.

cautious or inconclusive opinions as it may not be possible to differentiate between the awkward writing conditions associated with certain e-signing environments and simulation. There are many limiting factors to consider when comparing an electronic signature to samples of pen-and-paper signatures. These limiting factors include the differences in writing surface and writing instrument as well as the quality in which the signature was electronically recorded. While some qualified opinions may be possible, unqualified opinions are probably not advisable, and inconclusive opinions may be the most reliable opinion in certain cases.

For other types of examinations, such as the comparison of a disputed electronic signature to a set of recorded electronic signature samples, the analysis is dependent upon the sophistication of the data captured and available for analysis. Some handwriting verification systems perform an automated analysis of the signature. Others provide biometric data that can be independently examined. There are verification systems that advertise various claims, such as "forgery proof," which are questionable claims at best, especially given the considerable variables involved in handwriting examination. While proficiency among forensic document examiners in signature examination has been established in the academic literature, not all handwriting variables have been independently tested (Found et al., 2001; Kam et al., 2001). Computerized handwriting analysis has also received academic recognition, but again, not all variables have been tested (Srihari et al., 2002). Certain variables that need further research in forensic handwriting identification include health factors, effect of medications, whether a person is left-handed or right-handed, and intentional disguise on the part of the signer, to name a few. It is difficult to imagine that commercially available handwriting verification systems have taken the considerable research time necessary to account for all handwriting variables, let alone the problems inherent in a writer's natural range of variation. For example, if a handwriting verification system recorded a minimum number of base comparison signatures (such as five), this number may not be sufficient for verification, especially since most forensic document examiners require more than five signatures for the purposes of comparison. Additionally, there may be an unintended training effect associated with the collection of signatures for verification in a signature security system. In order to pass the "test," the person signing may adapt to an unnaturally consistent version of his or her signature. This could have potential implications, because it might assist in the ease of forgery, rather than hindering forgery.

5.7 LEGAL IMPLICATIONS

The legal field may need knowledge about the vast array of forensic problems that could be presented by digital and electronic signatures. Some of the claims made by companies manufacturing and distributing electronic and biometric signature systems may be overconfident in their assertions. Some manufacturers claim their systems are 100% forgery-proof, some claim their systems are forensically identifiable (even though a mouse is used to produce the signature), while others state that it is impossible for their verification systems to pass a forgery. The concern with these new technologies is that the end-user may have too much confidence in a system that may not have considered all the variables associated with handwriting (and there are many) and the other variables associated with online signing that have not been adequately researched.

A recent *Daubert* ruling in a U.S. district court underscores the need for document examiners to define the best evidence available when handling biometric electronic signature cases. In *American Family Life Assurance Company of Columbus (AFLAC) v. Glenda Biles* (2011), the defendant Biles claimed that signatures of the deceased had been forged on an insurance application and arbitration acknowledgment forms. The defendant retained a document examiner expert, who was provided with a hard copy of the documents. The plaintiff, AFLAC, retained an expert who was provided with the digital data of the dynamic, electronic signature associated with the disputed documents. Motions to dismiss the affidavits produced by both experts were filed by the respective parties, and a *Daubert* hearing was conducted of each side's expert. The evidence provided by defendant's expert was deemed to be unreliable by the court.

In the court's memorandum, it was noted that the plaintiff's insurance agent had witnessed the deceased sign the contested signatures on a Topaz electronic signature pad. AFLAC contested that the defendant's expert had relied on a low-resolution static image of the disputed signatures that was not an accurate representation of the data recorded. The defendant's expert admitted that initially he had not realized that he was examining a dynamic electronic signature nor did he subsequently examine the digital data that was available. The court found that the defendant's expert did not rely on the best evidence available, while the document examination expert for AFLAC relied on the digital data of the disputed signatures. The court granted the motion to strike the affidavit of the defendant's expert and granted the plaintiff's motion for summary judgment.

The *AFLAC* ruling clearly demonstrates that static images of electronic signatures are not considered the best evidence available, and that testimony based on such evidence may be considered unreliable. In the court's memorandum, it was stated that the plaintiff's expert compared the recorded signature data to known exemplars of the deceased's signatures. The court did not mention in its ruling whether these comparison samples were also electronically recorded signatures nor does the court's ruling state the reasons for the defendant's motion to dismiss the plaintiff expert's affidavit. The court was justified in its finding that the plaintiff's expert relied on the best evidence available. However, if the plaintiff's expert was comparing dynamic electronic signatures to ink-and-paper signatures, the question remains whether the best evidence available was forensically reliable evidence to make claims regarding authenticity.

5.8 PROPOSED METHODOLOGY

Clearly, the challenges faced by forensic document examiners concerning dynamic signatures require collaboration with computer forensics. The problems involved in the forensic analysis of dynamic, electronic signatures highlight the need to work within a framework such as computational forensics. Computational forensics is the application of a methodology to help quantify and standardize forensic analysis (Franke & Srihari, 2007; Srihari, 2010). Automatic signature verification techniques can aid handwriting examiners by providing statistical analyses and standardizing work processes. Other standardized guidelines for forensic collection and analysis of electronic evidence are outlined by Mason (2010). These types of processes and guidelines would be useful for forensic document examiners to incorporate when handling electronic signature cases.

Further, forensic document examiner research in conjunction with computer forensics is necessary to more clearly define thresholds related to minimum levels of forensically reliable data. In working with dynamic, electronic signature technology, forensic document examiners need more than access to the best evidence available; they also need an understanding concerning the limitations of signatures captured with too little information.

In establishing standards, a method for the forensic analysis of electronic handwritten signatures is proposed. Figure 5.15 shows a flow chart for a visual application of the method. The methodology is broken down into three major categories that are based upon the types of signatures in which a forensic document examiner may be consulted: (1) digital cryptographic signature; (2) biometric handwritten signature; and (3) and static handwritten signature.

While the first category involving digital cryptographic signatures is beyond the scope of most forensic handwriting experts, as it does not involve a physical "handwriting" process, it is still mentioned as part of the methodology because it represents a limitation in the scope of work of forensic handwriting experts. Document examiners receive analysis

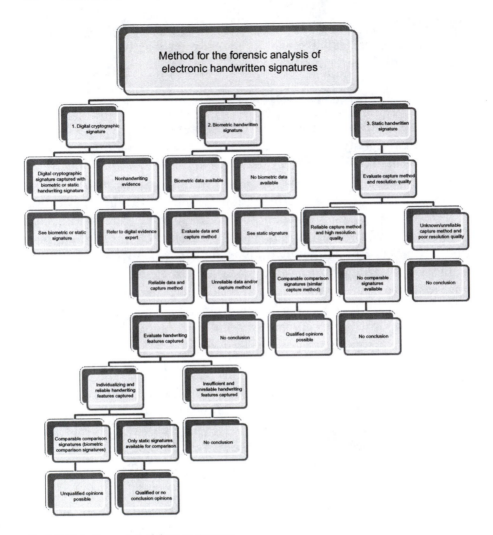

Fig. 5.15 Method for analysis of electronic signatures.

requests from investigators and attorneys about cryptographic-based "signatures" so it is important to include these digital algorithms as part of the methodology and their subsequent limitations for handwriting experts. Forensic document examiners can educate themselves about the security requirements for digital signatures and their analysis so as to give clients and investigators more informed advice about their analysis and refer to a digital evidence specialist. It is also important for document examiners to know how a digital signature may be a part of the digital signing process as digital signatures and electronic handwritten signatures are sometimes used together in signing a document. In these instances, digital evidence specialists and forensic handwriting examiners may need to work together in the document analysis. It is also recommended that document examiners have a broad understanding of digital signatures so that they can guide clients about the correct type of analysis. Laypersons may not know the difference between digital signatures and handwritten electronic signatures. Sometimes digital and handwritten electronic signatures are created together on the same document.

A handwritten biometric signature involves the capture of computerized data, usually a combination of online and offline characteristics. If no biometric characteristics have been captured, but there is a graphic representation of a handwritten signature presented for analysis, then the examiner needs to treat the signature as a static signature. Additionally, even if it is known that biometric data was captured but has not been presented to the examiner or is for some reason unavailable, the examiner still needs to limit the opinion according to the guidelines for static signatures. When biometric data is available, the examiner should also make inquiries about how the data was stored and transmitted in order to ensure that the data is reliable. An inquiry about the signing conditions (tablet and stylus used) in addition to the quality of the data (hertz rate) is all a part of the analysis and should be reflected by the level of opinion provided.

The next phase of the analysis of biometric signatures involves handwriting feature analysis. At this stage, the examiner evaluates the individualizing character of the captured handwriting features as well as their reliability both in terms of standards already established in forensic handwriting examination and what research has informed us about online biometric features. There are numerous features that can be used in analysis, but research has shown that certain characteristics are more consistent and reliable than others (see Section 5.4). Insufficient or unreliable handwriting characteristics would result in an inconclusive opinion, especially if there were no comparable specimens available for comparison. It has been noted by researchers and developers of handwriting verification systems that one characteristic alone is not sufficient to establish handwriting identification; it is the combination of characteristics that establishes identification (Franke et al., 2004; Srihari et al., 2002).

Even if the questioned signature is a sophisticated biometric, the comparison signatures also need to be comparable to the questioned signature. Just as in any forensic signature case, the number of comparison samples need to be adequate, contemporaneous, and written under similar conditions. So, if the biometric signature was written with a finger on a touchpad, the comparison signatures also need to be written in a similar way. Some systems have a database of signatures used for enrollment, but many of these systems only capture a few signatures, which may not be adequate depending on handwriting factors such as complexity and range of variation. When there are a sufficient number of biometric signatures available and captured under similar conditions, the dynamic and static features available in biometric signatures can allow for conclusive opinions. When only static signatures are available for comparative analysis (these may be digitized or pen-and-paper signatures), qualified opinions may be possible especially if a stylus was used in creating the biometric signature. The static signatures also need to be evaluated for quality of image.

The third signature type, static handwritten signatures, can also be referred to as digitized signatures. These signatures are captured on an electronic device, but no biometric data or computer files are associated with the digitized image. The examiner may receive the signature either as a digitized electronic page (such as a PDF file with an image of the signature on the document) or as a hard copy print out. Because of the digital manipulation that can occur with these signatures, it may not be possible to conclusively associate the signature with the document and the examiner may be limited to making opinions about the handwriting characteristics of the signature only. Evaluating the resolution quality of the signature is important. Any digitized signature encountered by an examiner should be evaluated for electronic signature production. Sometimes examiners receive hard copies of questioned signatures not realizing that the questioned signature had been written with an electronic device. If the signature was signed on a device and then transferred and embedded onto the document, the digitized signature may have an awkward or unnatural size with respect to the signature space on the document. The signature may also not interact with the baseline or surrounding signature area. Signatures that are embedded onto documents may also be reduced in size. A digitized signature with poor resolution (highly pixelated) and limited handwriting characteristics should be evaluated with caution, and inconclusive opinions are recommended. High resolution quality in combination with comparison signatures captured in a similar electronic environment can yield qualified opinions.

This proposed method focuses only on the parameters related to digital and electronic handwriting variables. The method should be used in conjunction with other established handwriting examination standards and methods such as ASTM Standard E2290-07: a Standard Guide for Examination of Handwritten Items (2007) and the modular approach to handwriting identification developed by Found & Rogers (1999b). As research into electronic signatures develops, this proposed method would naturally need to adopt relevant research findings and emerging technology especially as it establishes thresholds related to resolution quality and more conclusively identifies individualizing and reliable online and offline handwriting features.

5.9 SUMMARY

The advent of the electronic signature challenges forensic analysts to analyze the digitally produced data of signatures in new ways. Temporal, dynamic data related to the speed and pressure of the signature can now be captured and quantified, data that is only estimated by examiners when examining the static trace from pen and ink signatures. The biometric information from signatures is used in biometric-based security systems. Some of the new considerations in forensic assessment not only involve computerized, electronic data but also the hardware involved with signing e-signatures, such as the stylus and the tablet. Evaluation of electronic signature systems shows that there is a wide variety of systems on the market, not only in the capture of e-signatures but also in their automated forensic analysis. Lack of standardization from both a capture and verification perspective complicates forensic analysis of these types of signatures. The ruling from a recent legal case demonstrated that forensic document examiners need to be alert to the fact that examining electronic signatures from static trace images alone is not considered the best evidence available in e-signature cases when biometric data is available. It is recommended that document examiners collaborate with computer evidence specialists and work within a methodological framework. A recommended methodology for examining digital and electronic signatures is proposed.

CHAPTER 6

The Law, Science, and Handwriting Identification

Forensic handwriting identification has made significant progress toward its establishment as a scientifically valid and reliable science. As in any science, further research and standardization is necessary, and this is ongoing in the field, but the field has been able to successfully meet challenges concerning scientific admissibility in the court room.

In this chapter, we provide an overview of scientific challenges to forensic handwriting identification as outlined in the National Research Council of the National Academies of Science (NAS) report concerning forensic reform, which has been extensively disseminated in the media and in the legal field (2009). The NAS report's critical summary of forensic handwriting identification was previously reviewed by Harralson (2010) and is updated here.

6.1 FORENSIC SCIENCE REFORM

In 2005, the US Congress commissioned the NAS to examine critical forensic science issues including challenges facing the various forensic specialties, disparities and fragmentation in the forensic science community, lack of mandatory standardization, certification, accreditation, interpretation of forensic evidence, the need for research, and the legal admissibility of forensic science evidence. The National Research Council of the NAS publicized its report to Congress in early 2009, titled "Strengthening Forensic Science in the United States: A Path Forward." There has been widespread media attention on the NAS report, and several conferences and meetings at law schools were conducted throughout the United States to publicize the report's recommendations to the legal community.

The overriding message of the NAS report is that forensic science has failed to meet the demands of science. Essentially, the committee calls for an overhaul of the practice and procedures of most forensic science disciplines including fingerprint analysis, toolmark and firearms identification, questioned document examination, hair and fiber evidence, and shoeprints and tire tracks. Some of the recommendations are not surprising in light of the negative media attention that crime laboratories and accrediting agencies have received over the years with respect to errors and procedural problems involving forensic evidence.

The NAS committee proposes several recommendations to improve forensic science:

1. Establish an independent federal entity, the National Institute of Forensic Sciences (NIFS), to oversee and establish standards, research, forensic practices, education, certification, accreditation, and development of technology.
2. Establish standard terminology and reporting procedures.
3. Conduct research to address issues of accuracy, reliability, and validity.
4. Remove public forensic laboratories from the administrative control of law enforcement agencies or prosecutors' offices.
5. Conduct research on human observer bias and sources of human error.
6. Develop tools for measurement, validation, reliability, information sharing, and proficiency to ensure quality control and best practices.
7. Require mandatory enforcement of forensic scientist certification and laboratory accreditation.
8. Establish quality assurance and quality control procedures.
9. Require mandatory enforcement of a national code of ethics.
10. Develop academic-level education and training programs.

As a response to the NAS report, Senator Patrick Leahy introduced legislation in early 2011 regarding forensic science reform whose function is "to establish an Office of Forensic Science and a Forensic Science Board, to strengthen and promote confidence in the criminal justice system by ensuring consistency and scientific validity in forensic testing, and for other purposes" (p. 1). The senate bill outlines the responsibilities of a Forensic Science Board toward structure and oversight, accreditation of laboratories, certification, research, and standards.

6.2 A CRITICAL REVIEW OF FORENSIC HANDWRITING EXAMINATION

In reviewing specific forensic disciplines, the NAS committee points out that several forensic disciplines are "experience-based methods of pattern recognition" which include analysis of friction ridge, footwear and tire impressions, toolmarks, and handwriting (National Research Council of the National Academies, 2009, pp. 5–7). Although the review of questioned document examination covered the examination of ink and the sampling problems that can occur with ink examinations, the focus was on handwriting examination. Specifically, issues with respect to handwriting variability (interpersonal variability compared to intrapersonal variability) were addressed. Essentially, the NAS committee recognizes the need for more scientific research in handwriting examination:

Display Quote

The scientific basis for handwriting comparisons needs to be strengthened. Recent studies have increased our understanding of the individuality and consistency of handwriting and computer studies and suggest that there may be a scientific basis for handwriting comparison, at least in the absence of intentional obfuscation or forgery. Although there has been only limited research to quantify the reliability and replicability of the practices used by trained document examiners, the committee agrees that there may be some value in handwriting analysis. (pp. 5–30)

The NAS report cites three studies recognizing the scientific basis for handwriting comparison (Kam et al., 1997; Sita et al., 2002; Srihari et al., 2002); however, the committee comments that the scientific basis for handwriting comparison needs to be strengthened. The committee also points out that according to two of the cited studies, forensic document examiners had erroneous rates of 6.5% (Kam et al., 1997) and 3.4% (Sita et al., 2002), respectively. The NAS committee recognizes the work by Srihari et al. which addressed the individuality of handwriting.

The message conveyed in an NAS report conference (Risinger, 2009) is that handwriting examination has value, but research needs to go beyond signature identification and into problematic areas so as to ascertain the limitations of the science. Risinger (2007) comments that the court needs to take the *Kumho Tire* approach and focus its attention on addressing the "task at hand" to ensure that the task has been subjected to reliability and validity studies (pp. 463–464). He reviews handwriting tasks that have been proffered for testimony in court to illustrate how many of these handwriting tasks have not been subjected to scientific validity and reliability tests. Since the *Daubert* decision, handwriting identification "expertise has turned up in about 300 reported cases, including about 120 in federal court and 180 in state court. In only one reported state case, so far as the record reflects, was a challenge made to the validity of any part of document examiner handwriting identification practice. In federal court, nine such reported challenges have been made and litigated pursuant to *Daubert* (which resulted in ten opinions), and in two of those cases substantial restrictions were placed upon the scope of such handwriting identification testimony" (Risinger, 2006, pp. 139–140). The point Risinger makes in his review of these cases is that handwriting identification is not being adequately challenged in court. Merlino et al. (2007) evaluated federal cases in which document examination expert testimony was excluded and found that the exclusion was based on both expert qualifications and forensic document examination as a science. Regarding expert qualifications, judges specifically mentioned lack of: nonacademic training, skill with respect to subject matter, experience, publication record, and reputation as factors that precluded expert testimony. With respect to forensic document examination as a science, judges mentioned the lack of general acceptance, peer review and publication, known error rates, operating standards, consideration of alternative explanations, consistent theories/ findings, statistical significance, research purpose, and reliability as factors that precluded expert testimony.

The NAS committee urges that studies be conducted on human bias. Miller (1984) conducted a study about bias in handwriting identification cases comparing two groups of student document examiners. The first group was presented with a case that included leading and contextual information about the case and the handwriting of only one suspect. The second group was provided with the same case and the handwriting of three suspects. More than half the students in the first group came to an erroneous conclusion whereas the students in the second group were 100% accurate. Other studies examining forensic science bias have shown similar results (Dror & Charlton, 2006; Dror et al., 2006; Miller, 1987).

6.3 STATUS OF FORENSIC HANDWRITING IDENTIFICATION

The NAS report and critics of forensic science make valuable recommendations that need attention by forensic practitioners. While improvements in procedures and research are absolutely essential, it seems that the establishment of certifying bodies and methodologies as well as some of the research that has been conducted, may have been overlooked by the committee. In some of the problematic areas addressed by the NAS report, document examiners have already addressed or are currently addressing many of these weaknesses. Critical areas are reviewed to assess what document examiners are doing, or could be doing, to further support the scientific underpinnings of some of their tasks, such as handwriting identification in areas such as education, certification, proficiency testing, scientific validity and reliability, terminology and methodology standardization, and advances in technology.

6.4 EDUCATION AND TRAINING

The education and training of document examiners needs an academic focus, with emphasis on the sciences. According to Risinger (2006), "handwriting identification witnesses have generally been "technicians"—persons without any academic background in the sciences (and rarely with graduate degrees) who have received apprenticeship training in handwriting examination" (p. 141). The NAS committee agrees and states that "the forensic science enterprise...is hindered by its extreme disaggregation—marked by multiple types of practitioners with different levels of education and training and different professional cultures and standards for performance and a reliance on apprentice-type training and a guild-like structure of disciplines, which work against the goal of a single forensic science profession" (NRCNAS 2009, p. S-11). While it is true, historically, that most document examiners did not have academic backgrounds in the sciences, this is changing as industry standards are becoming more clearly defined. Currently, the ASTM training standard (E2388-11) requires an undergraduate degree for all document examiners trained subsequent to its publication. However, this degree does not have to be in a related science. The actual training (according to the standard) is still based on a two-year apprenticeship-type model. The current standard, while acknowledging the importance of an undergraduate degree, needs revision in order to reflect the academic training standards and requirements proposed by the NAS committee.

New academic programs in the forensic sciences are changing the apprenticeship model. Many forensic science degrees are available in universities at both undergraduate and graduate levels. To meet the needs for an academic program in forensic document examination, East Tennessee State University (ETSU) began offering a graduate certificate degree in forensic document examination. This program is accessible to students throughout the United States and internationally, provided they have an undergraduate degree. A Master of Science in Forensic Science with an emphasis on forensic document examination and a graduate certificate degree are available through Oklahoma State University (OSU). While both ETSU and OSU offer accessible online programs, forensic document examination programs of OSU are restricted to students recommended by members of the American Society of Questioned Document Examiners (ASQDE) or the American Board of Forensic Document Examiners (ABFDE). With respect to other training opportunities, Merlino et al. (2007) list several universities in the United States offering document examination courses within forensic science programs. The availability of courses and programs in forensic document examination at universities is an important step toward meeting the NAS committee's recommendation for academic training in the field. Because of the trend for universities to offer forensic programs online, the ASTM forensic document examination training standard (E2388-11) needs revision in order to reflect recent advances in academic training and distance learning.

6.5 CERTIFICATION AND LABORATORY ACCREDITATION

With respect to certification and laboratory accreditation, the NAS report discusses the fragmentation of the forensic sciences field and forensic document examination is no exception. To address this problem, the Forensic Specialties Accreditation Board (FSAB), with support and assistance from the American Academy of Forensic Sciences, the National Forensic Science Technology Center, and the National Institute of Justice, established a board to accredit forensic specialty certification boards. While FSAB accreditation is not mandatory at this time, it is an important step toward the consolidation and unification of certification in the forensic sciences. In the field of forensic document examination there are several programs, schools, and organizations offering certification. Currently, only two of these boards are accredited by FSAB: the Board of Forensic Document Examiners (BFDE) and the ABFDE. FSAB requires comprehensive testing, adherence to a professional code of ethics, and continuing education. As of 2005, FSAB required that the accredited boards comply with ASTM E2388-05, the training guide for forensic document examiners, which requires an undergraduate degree.

Laboratory accreditation is offered by the American Society of Crime Laboratory Directors/Laboratory Accreditation Board (ASCLD/LAB) and Forensic Quality Services International (FQS-I). Siegel (2009) commented that there should be mandatory accreditation of all public and private laboratories, including private laboratories employing a single forensic expert. At this time, there is no practical mechanism to accredit small, private sector laboratories. Additionally, because of highly publicized problems with crime laboratories, laboratory accrediting agencies have also received criticism. Clearly, this is an area that needs further attention.

6.6 PROFICIENCY TESTING

Proficiency testing is available through Collaborative Testing Services (CTS), which offers an annual test on handwriting identification and another test on some other technical aspects of document examination. For several years, LaTrobe University in Australia offered proficiency testing in handwriting identification to participants internationally through its Forensic Expertise Profiling Laboratory (FEPL) program. The results of many of LaTrobe's proficiency examinations were published in peer-reviewed journals and symposium proceedings, which has helped to establish and characterize forensic handwriting examiner skill in a variety of handwriting tasks. Skill-Task Training Assessment

& Research, Inc. (ST²AR), based in the United States, in collaboration with researchers at LaTrobe University, currently offers proficiency testing in handwriting and document examination. The ST²AR program is continuing the proficiency research that was originally initiated by researchers at LaTrobe University.

6.7 SCIENTIFIC VALIDITY AND RELIABILITY

Statistical studies that have been conducted on handwriting identification lend support to its scientific validity. Studies have shown that handwriting is unique and identifiable (Lytle & Yang, 2006; Marquis et al., 2005; Srihari et al., 2002, 2008). Other studies have statistically explored range of variation to identify and quantify intra-writer variation (Jindal et al., 1999; Ling, 2002; Marquis et al., 2005). Statistical probability on the uniqueness of identifiable characteristics was conducted by Zimmerman (1998). Statistical methods that can be used by examiners have been proposed by Strach (1998) and Found et al. (1994).

Regarding the scientific reliability of opinions offered by practitioners, studies published in peer-reviewed journals have proved the ability of document examiners to distinguish between genuine and simulated handwriting and to match handwriting samples (Found & Rogers, 2003; Found et al., 1999b, 2001; Kam & Lin, 2003; Kam et al., 1994, 1997, 2001; Sita et al., 2002). Compiling the error rates from the published studies, document examiner error rates were in the range of 0.04–9.3%. Some of the studies also showed that document examiners exhibited more skill than laypersons in performing handwriting identification (layperson error rates were in the range of 26.1–42.86%).

The research published thus far has demonstrated document examiner reliability on tasks including both handwriting and signatures, including detection of simulations produced by expert penmen (Dewhurst et al., 2008) and distinguishing between simulation and disguise (Bird et al., 2010b; Found & Rogers, 2007). These studies have helped to define when caution needs to be exercised in expressing handwriting opinions. More research is required and is ongoing with respect to problematic handwriting tasks. Until that research is conducted and experts are proficiency tested on a wide variety of difficult tasks, the *Kumho Tire v. Carmichael* (1999) ruling that advises expert acceptance based on a review of the "task at hand" is prudent.

6.8 TERMINOLOGY AND METHODOLOGY

In the field of forensic document examination, ASTM Subcommittee E30.02 on Questioned Documents has published several standards covering subjects such as general terminology, opinion language, handwriting examination procedures, examining documents for alterations, ink comparison, paper, and other document examination topics. Another organization that publishes standards is SWGDOC. SWGDOC is sponsored by the FBI and funded by government agencies. It was assigned the task of writing laboratory Standard Operating Procedures (SOPs) into standards so there would be procedural consistency among public laboratories. Membership in the SWGDOC group is limited to those who have been trained in or are working in the public sector. The ASTM, on the other hand, is an organization open to all professionals within the field, and standards are developed by consensus of the membership. Membership includes those trained both in the public and in the private sectors.

In addition to the ASTM and SWGDOC standards, methodological procedures on the examination and analysis of handwriting have been published by Slyter (1995) and Found & Rogers (1999). Slyter developed specific criteria for formulating levels of opinion based on a methodological and hierarchical analysis of comparison elements. The methodology included rating and evaluating the limitations in comparison material. Found & Rogers developed a method flow diagram for handwriting examination that incorporates decision-making about alternative propositions prior to reaching the opinion formation stage(s). The method flow diagram proposes a method of examination to ensure that the examiner carefully evaluates alternative explanations and limitations (e.g., contamination of standards, comparability, altered neurophysiology, altered environmental conditions, and complexity) prior to proposing an authorship opinion.

6.9 ADVANCES IN HANDWRITING IDENTIFICATION TECHNOLOGY

Computerized software systems have been developed, such as FISH (Franke et al., 2003) and CEDAR-FOX (Srihari et al., 2008). These systems rely on handwriting databases, enable automated examination features, and produce statistical analyses. The FBI, through the coordinated efforts of scientists and computer engineers, developed the Forensic Language-Independent Automated System for Handwriting

Identification (FLASH-ID). The system employs Gannon's FLEX-Tracker handwriting biometric system (Gannon Technologies Group, 2008). Although not meant to replace forensic handwriting examiners, computerized methods of analysis help with establishing statistical support for expert opinions. These computerized systems for handwriting identification may be likened to the Automated Fingerprint Identification System (AFIS) used by fingerprint examiners where a latent fingerprint is compared to known inked impressions in a database. Like AFIS, the handwriting computerized systems also require a forensic examiner to make a personal examination of possible matches resulting from the computerized system. In many ways, though, an automated handwriting identification system is more complex than AFIS due to the greater degree of variables that are an inherent part of handwriting. Biometric identifiers are used in the system, and, according to the FBI (2007), only the essential biometric identifiers, known as the Biometric Kernel, are relied upon in making matches within the system. Using statistical algorithms across several handwriting features, statistical matches are made to writings already in the database. Using what Gannon (2011) refers to as graph-based recognition technology, the accuracy rate for writer identification is 98% in a text with as few as 50 words. FLASH-ID uses a loss-less data structure that ensures the integrity of the original graphic handwriting features. The system is also language independent relying on graphical rather than linguistical features. The FBI conservatively points out, though, that the system is not designed to replace document examiners, only to capture and process data much more rapidly while offering statistical analysis in a way that has not been previously possible in forensic handwriting examination.

A few studies have compared the accuracy of automatic handwriting verification systems to forensic handwriting experts. One study compared performance between automated systems and handwriting experts but had difficulty comparing expertise because equal error rates (EERs) cannot be calculated for human experts (Liwicki et al., 2010). In a difficult handwriting task, the handwriting examiners had 7.2% misleading opinions while 52.3% of the opinions were inconclusive. For the same task, automatic handwriting verification systems (seven in total) had a combined average EER of 66.1.

In a study on differentiating the handwriting of twins, an automatic handwriting verification system's performance was compared to that of document examination interns and laypersons. By comparison, the system had an error rate of 9.02%, document examination intern error rate was 4.69%, while layperson error rate was 16.51% (Srihari et al., 2008). It was demonstrated that the automatic handwriting verification system's performance was better than laypersons' but less than that of document examiners.

6.10 LEGAL CHALLENGES TO SCIENTIFIC ADMISSIBILITY

Almost as an answer to the criticism aimed at forensic handwriting examination, a recent court case originating in the District of Columbia Court of Appeals challenged forensic handwriting examination using criticisms taken from the NAS report. In *Pettus v. United States* (2012), the appellant, Pettus, protested that "the trial judge erroneously admitted the expert opinion of an FBI forensic document examiner that a piece of handwriting left on the body of the murder victim had been written by the appellant" (pp. 1–2). An envelope was found on the victim's body containing a short handwritten note that was purportedly written by the appellant. This was compared to several pages of the appellant's known handwriting. The FBI's forensic document examiner testified that there were no significant differences between the writings but rather that there were "significant combinations of handwriting characteristics" between the known and questioned writing (p. 4). Principally, the appellant's argument was based upon the NAS report's criticism that forensic pattern-based disciplines are not scientific and do not meet the requirements for scientific admissibility. The appellate court agreed with the original trial court's decision that handwriting identification did indeed meet the *Frye* test for admissibility. The court further reasoned that the appellant's presentation of the criticism from the NAS report "exaggerates the measured conclusions and recommendations of the Report to read them as a rejection of the scientific basis for all pattern-matching analysis, including handwriting identification" (p. 27). Rather, the court found that the NAS report does not recommend a rejection of handwriting identification but instead cautions courts to insist on reliability of forensic methods. Overall, the appellate court found that the NAS report did not specify a reason for rejecting handwriting identification, noting that the NAS report's review of handwriting identification was brief. The court concluded that the methodology behind handwriting identification is well established and accepted in the forensic community.

6.11 SUMMARY

Since the *Daubert* hearing in *United States v. Starzecpyzel* (1995) when handwriting identification received its first real challenge as a science, forensic document examiners in both the public and the private sectors have taken on increased responsibility for meeting the challenges presented by the NAS recommendations. Many document examiners in both the public and the private sectors have been certified under the FSAB guidelines for accreditation of certification programs, have participated in proficiency testing, maintained scientific methodology and training standards, and have participated in and promoted research in validity and reliability studies. The important work that has been accomplished over the past several years has propelled the field toward scientific acceptance. Arguments from the NAS report were used to challenge forensic handwriting examination in the District of Columbia Court of Appeals case *Pettus v. United States* but were successfully denied as the court found that handwriting identification meets the requirements of scientific admissibility.

Acceleration: Handwriting features which shows change or increase in velocity or speed; the rate in which handwriting changes velocity.

Air Stroke: Handwriting movements that are recorded while the pen is lifted above the digital tablet surface. Air strokes are not visible in the static handwriting trace but can be observed in the recorded handwriting movements.

Artificial Neural Network (ANN): Used for finding patterns in handwriting data. In computer science, they are adaptive, interconnected systems that change structure through machine learning techniques.

Altitude: Handwriting feature related to the steepness or height of the pen.

Azimuth: Handwriting feature related to the direction of the pen on to the writing plane.

Biometric Signature: Electronically recorded signature or handwriting that captures temporal dynamics and spatial properties. Handwriting process and product are captured simultaneously. Handwriting features such as pen pressure and duration of the signing process, which is done with a stylus on a display screen, or digital pen tablet, is recorded and can be compared against future signatures (see **Dynamic, Temporal**).

Curvature-Ellipse: Handwriting feature related to curve radius.

Digital Ink: Some digital pad devices have active displays which show the handwriting trace on the electronic display at the pen and time location at or near real time. The trace on the display is referred to as digital ink.

Digital Signature: A mathematical algorithm comprised of a private key and public key that is used for authenticating an electronic document. Digital signatures are mathematical data, not handwritten signatures.

Digital Tablet: A computer input device that enables the user to draw, write, or sign a signature in a way similar to writing on paper with a pen or pencil. The tablet serves as the "paper" surface. Writing on the tablet allows for the digitization of the drawing, writing, or signature (also Computer Tablet, Digitizer, Digitizing Tablet, Drawing Tablet, Graphics Tablet).

Dynamic: Refers to electronically captured temporal handwriting features such as velocity, pressure, and duration. The dynamics of the signature refer to the movement patterns of the handwriting.

Dynamic Time Warping (DTW): Used in online signature recognition. The algorithm measures similarity between two sequences when there are variances in time between the sequences. For example, if there were differences in time between two handwriting sequences, written by the same person, similarities in the handwriting sequences could still be detected. Time is warped in one signature so that two recorded handwriting patterns optimally resemble each other, both in space and time.

Electronic Signature: Handwritten signature that is captured on an electronic device using a stylus and digital tablet, or a digital pen. The law does not distinguish between a digital algorithm signature and a biometric signature. They are both considered electronic signatures even though they are different "signing" processes (also E-signature).

Enrollment: Phase in automatic handwriting verification when reference or known signatures are entered into the system. The enrolled signatures are compared to future signatures entered into the system, usually for the purposes of access or entry into a system.

Equal Error Rate (EER): In probability statistics, error rates are used in biometric systems to determine the accuracy of the system for false acceptance rate (FAR) and false rejection rate (FRR). The EER is calculated as the balance between the FAR and the FRR. The lower the EER, the more accurate the system.

Facsimile: A copy of a document that is transmitted telephonically or digitally (also Fax).

Fast Fourier Transform (FFT): An efficient algorithm used in digital signal processing of handwriting where a sequence of N x and y positions (N must be power of 2) are transformed into a set of N harmonious waves each with its own frequency and phase.

Feature Extraction: Features are extracted from large amounts of data resulting in a major reduction of data. Used in pattern recognition and the image processing phase of the handwriting verification process.

Feature Vector: An ordered set of different features. The mathematical space associated with a feature in extraction of handwriting features. The feature or associated image may be represented by pixels.

Freehand Simulation: A simulation method involving the attempted imitation of a handwriting or signature based upon an available model handwriting. The simulation is performed through memory of the model or observation of the model.

Forgery: A legal term implying the intent to defraud (see **Simulation**).

Frequency Spectrum: Output of the Fast Fourier Transform often represented as the amplitude of the harmonious waves as a function of frequency. The phase of the waves is normally neglected. The frequency spectrum is thus the square root of the power spectrum. The informative part runs from frequency 0 till half the sampling frequency.

Gaussian Mixture Models (GMMs): Statistical method used for clustering and density estimation.

Global Feature: Handwriting feature extracted for the entire signature unit.

Hash Function: Cryptographic function associated with digital signatures. The hash reduces the data from a variable length to a fixed length.

Hertz (Hz): A unit of frequency. For example, the number of cycles or periods per second of the harmonious waves in handwriting or the number of samples per second when recording handwriting.

Hidden Markov Model (HMM): A statistical tool for modeling a linear sequence based on a Markov process. Because it is a probabilistic model, it can be linked to Bayesian theory. HMM is frequently used for modeling temporal patterns in biometrics where there can be latent or hidden variables such as in handwriting and speech recognition.

Interpolation: The creation of new data points in between known data points.

Kinematic: The physics of motion in handwriting.

Local Feature: Handwriting feature based on a single data point.

Noise: Variations or disturbances during transmission of analog data before it is digitized which can cause interference or degradation of the handwriting recording.

Offline: Handwriting or signature written with pen on paper. Also refers to the analysis of a static signature. Some electronically captured signatures may be analyzed through their graphic, static forms without the aid of temporal data (see **Static**).

Online: Handwriting or signature written using handwriting capture technology. In capturing an "online" signature, temporal, dynamic characteristics are recorded such as duration and velocity (see **Dynamic**, **Temporal**).

Optical Character Recognition (OCR): In handwriting, conversion of handwritten characters or images into computer text.

Pen Computing: Use of a stylus, instead of a mouse or keyboard, for interfacing with computers, either on a PC Tablet or through a digital tablet.

Private Key: Part of the digital signature algorithm that locks or encrypts data.

Public Key: Part of the digital signature algorithm that opens or unlocks encrypted data.

Simulation: The attempt to copy or imitate the handwriting or signature of another person.

Static: Handwriting produced using pen-and-paper methods, with no online data captured. Static signatures can also be digitized versions of electronic signatures (see **Offline**).

Temporal: Refers to the movement and speed factors involved with the handwriting features extracted from biometric signatures such as duration, speed, and velocity (see **Dynamic**, **Online**).

Time Derivative: Rate of change of the value of a function.

Torque: Dynamic handwriting feature related to rotational force.

Tracing: A method of handwriting simulation that copies directly from a model using transmitted light, indentation, or impression.

Velocity: The vector describing both speed and direction of the handwriting stroke. It can be described by a horizontal or x-coordinate and a vertical or y-coordinate.

Wet Ink: A traditional signature signed with an inking pen on to paper. These types of signatures can be captured simultaneously with electronic signatures by having users sign with an electronic inking pen on to paper placed on top of a digital tablet (also Wet Signature).

x-Axis: Horizontal axis in the plane of the paper upon which the pen tip position is projected in recorded handwriting yielding a value for the x-coordinate.

y-Axis: Vertical axis in the plane of the paper upon which the pen tip position is projected in recorded handwriting yielding a value for the y-coordinate.

z-Axis: Axis perpendicular to the plane of the paper. The height of the pen above the paper can be expressed by the projection of the pen tip position on the z-axis. In practice, there are no pen movement recording devices that measure the pen height. Instead, most pen recording devices measure the axial pen pressure. This is the pressure exerted upon the pen tip along the direction of the pen barrel. Pen pressure is often treated as the z-coordinate.

REFERENCES

Afsar, F. A., Arif, M., & Farrukh, U. (2005). Wavelet transform based global features for online signature recognition. In *Proceedings of the ninth international multitopic conference, IEEE INMIC 2005*, December 2005 (pp. 1–6). Karachi, Pakistan.

Akamatsu, M., & MacKenzie, I. S. (2002). Changes in applied force to a touchpad during pointing tasks. *International Journal of Industrial Ergonomics, 29*(3), 171–182.

Akcin, N. (2012). The perspectives of primary school teachers on the evaluation and remediation of the compositions of students with learning disabilities. *American International Journal of Contemporary Research, 2*(3), 68–75.

Alonso-Fernandez, F., Fierrez-Aguilar, J., & Ortega-Garcia, J. (2005). Sensor interoperability and fusion in signature verification: A case study using tablet PC. *Advances in Biometric Person Authentication, Lecture Notes in Computer Science, 3781*, 180–187.

Alonso-Fernandez, F., Fierrez-Aguilar, J., & Ortega-Garcia, J. (2011). Quality measures in biometric systems. *Security and Privacy, IEEE Computer Society Digital Library, IEEE Computer Society* (pp. 99), 1.

Alpcan, T., Kesici, S., Bicher, D., Kivanc Mihcak, M., Bauckhage, C., & Ahmet Camtepe, S. (2008). A lightweight biometric signature scheme for user authentication over networks. In *Proceedings of the fourth international conference on security and privacy in communication networks*, September 22–25, 2008. Istanbul, Turkey. Retrieved from <http://dl.acm.org/citation.cfm?id=1460920>.

American Family Life Assurance Company of Columbus *(AFLAC) v. Glenda Biles*. (2011). WL 5325622 (S.D.Miss.). Retrieved from <http://law.justia.com/cases/federal/district-courts/mississippi/mssdce/3:2010cv00667/73831/80>.

American Standards for Testing and Materials International, ASTM E2290-07a (2007). Standard guide for examination of handwritten items. ASTM International, West Conshohocken, PA, DOI: 10.1520/E2290-07A, www.astm.org.

American Standards for Testing and Materials International, ASTM E2388-11 (2011). Standard guide for minimum training requirements for forensic document examiners. ASTM International, West Conshohocken, PA, DOI: 10.1520/E2388-11, www.astm.org.

Amma, C., Georgi, M., & Schultz, T. (2012). Airwriting: Hands-free mobile text input by spotting and continuous recognition of 3D-space handwriting with inertial sensors. In *Proceedings of the sixteenth international symposium on wearable computers (ISWC)*, June 18–22, 2012 (pp. 52–59). Newcastle, UK: Newcastle University.

Automated Signature Technology (2011). Ghostwriter: Easy to use, tough enough for any task. Retrieved from <http://www.signaturemachine.com/>.

Balestrino, M., Fontana, P., Terzuoli, S., Volpe, S., Inglese, M. L., & Cocito, L. (2012). Altered handwriting suggests cognitive impairment and may be relevant to posthumous evaluation. *Journal of Forensic Sciences, 57*(5), 1252–1258.

Ballard, L., Lopresti, D., & Monrose, F. (2006). Evaluating the security of handwriting biometrics. In *Tenth international workshop on frontiers in handwriting recognition*, October 2006. La Baule, France.

Barabe, J. G., Smith, K. J., & Florence, D. (2003). An introduction to ink analysis and characterization. *Journal of Forensic Document Examination, 15*, 49–72.

Bartolomeo, P., Bachoud-Lévi, A. C., Chokron, S., & Degos, J. D. (2002). Visually- and motor-based knowledge of letters: Evidence from a pure alexic patient. *Neuropsychologia, 40*(8), 1363–1371.

BBC News (February 26, 2009). The slow death of handwriting. Retrieved from <http://news.bbc.co.uk/2/hi/7907888.stm>.

Bechini, U. (2009). Bread and donkey for breakfast: How IT law false friends can confound lawmakers: An Italian tale about digital signatures. *Digital Evidence and Electronic Signature Law Review, 6*, 79–82.

Berninger, V. (2012). Evidence-based, developmentally appropriate writing skills K–5: Teaching the orthographic loop of working memory to write letters so developing writers can spell words and express ideas. Presented at *Handwriting in the twenty-first century? An educational summit* (January 23, 2012). Washington, DC.

Berninger, V. W., & Amtmann, D. (2003). In H. L. Swanson, K. R. Harris & S. Graham (Eds.), *Handbook of learning disabilities*. New York, NY: The Guilford Press.

Berninger, V. W., Vaughan, K., Graham, S., Abbott, R. D., Abbott, S. P., & Rogan, L. W., et al. (1997). Treatment of handwriting problems in beginning writers: Transfer from handwriting to composition. *Journal of Educational Psychology, 89*(4), 652–666.

Biary, N., & Koller, W. (1987). Kinetic predominant essential tremor: Successful treatment with clonazepam. *Neurology, 37*, 471–474.

Biometric Signature ID (BSI). (2012). Products and solutions. Retrieved from <http://www.biosig-id.com/products/>.

Bird, C., Found, B., Ballantyne, K., & Rogers, D. (2010b). Forensic document examiners' opinions on the process of production of disguised and simulated signatures. *Forensic Science International, 195*(1-3), 103–107.

Bird, C., Found, B., & Rogers, D. (2010a). Forensic document examiners' skill in distinguishing between natural and disguised handwriting behaviors. *Journal of Forensic Sciences, 55*(5), 1291–1295.

Birsh, J. R. (1999). *Multisensory teaching of basic language skills*. Baltimore, MD: Paul H. Brookes Publishing Co..

Boccignone, G., Chianese, A., Cordella, L. P., & Marcelli, A. (1993). Recovering dynamic information from static handwriting. *Pattern Recognition, 26*(3), 409–418.

Brink, A. A., Smit, J., Bulacu, M. L., & Schomaker, L. R. B. (2012). Writer identification using directional ink-trace width measurements. *Pattern Recognition, 45*(1), 162–171.

Bruinsma, C., & Nieuwenhuis, C. (1991). A new method for the evaluation of handwritten material. In J. Wann, A. M. Wing & N. Sovik (Eds.), *Development of graphic skills: Research, perspectives and educational implications*. San Diego, CA: Academic Press.

Brunelle, R. L., & Crawford, K. R. (2003). *Advances in the forensic analysis and date of writing ink*. Springfield, IL: Charles C. Thomas.

Brunelle, R. L., & Reed, R. W. (1984). *Forensic examination of ink and paper*. Springfield, IL: Charles C. Thomas.

Caligiuri, M. P., & Mohammed, L. A. (2012). *The neuroscience of handwriting: Applications for forensic document examination*. Boca Raton, FL: CRC Press.

Caligiuri, M. P., Teulings, H. -L., Dean, C. E., Niculescu, A. B., & Lohr, J. B. (2010). Handwriting movement kinematics for quantifying extrapyramidal side effects in patients treated with atypical antipsychotics. *Psychiatry Research, 177*(1), 77–83.

Case-Smith, J. (2012). Benefits of an OT/teacher model for first grade handwriting instruction. Presented at *Handwriting in the twenty-first century? An educational summit* (January 23, 2012). Washington, DC.

Causin, V., Casamassima, R., Marruncheddu, G., Lenzoni, G., Peluso, G., & Ripani, L. (2011). The discrimination potential of diffuse-reflectance ultraviolet-visible-near infrared spectrophotometry for the forensic analysis of paper. *Forensic Science International, 216*(1–3), 163–167.

Centers for Disease Control and Prevention (2011). Development disabilities increasing in US. Retrieved from <http://www.cdc.gov/features/dsdev_disabilities/index.html>.

Cha, S. -H., Tappert, C. C., Gibbons, M., & Chee, Y. -M. (2004). Automatic detection of handwriting forgery using a fractal number estimate of wrinkleless. *International Journal of Pattern Recognition and Artificial Intelligence, 18*(7), 1361–1371.

Conduit, R. (2008). The effect of sleep deprivation on the spatial characteristics of handwriting. *Journal of Forensic Document Examination, 19*, 29–39.

Conway, J. V. P. (1959). *Evidential documents.* Springfield, IL: Charles C. Thomas.

Coron, A. M., Stip, E., Dumont, C., & Lecours, A. R. (2000). Writing impairment in schizophasia: Two case studies. *Brain and Cognition, 43*, 121–124.

Dane-Elec Digital Products (2008). Dane-Elec Zpen. Retrieved from <http://www.danedigital.com/6-Zpen/>.

Daon (2011). EU secure VISA system launches using Daon software. Retrieved from <http://daon.com/content/eu-secure-visa-system-launches-using-daon-software>.

Daubert v. Merrell Dow Pharmaceuticals, Inc. (1993). 509 U.S. 113 579.

de Kerckhove, D., & Lumsden, C. J. (Eds.). (1988). *The alphabet and the brain: The lateralization of writing.* Berlin: Springer-Verlag.

Dewhurst, T., Found, B., & Rogers, D. (2008). Are expert penmen better than lay people at producing simulations of a model signature? *Forensic Science International, 180*(1), 50–53.

DocuSign, Inc. (2012). Retrieved from <http://www.docusign.com/>.

Doermann, D. S., & Rosenfeld, A. (1995). Recovery of temporal information from static images of handwriting. *International Journal of Computer Vision, 15*, 143–164.

Dror, I. E., & Charlton, D. (2006). Why experts make errors. *Journal of Forensic Identification, 56*(4), 600–616.

Dror, I. E., Charlton, D., & Peron, A. E. (2006). Contextual information renders experts vulnerable to making erroneous identifications. *Forensic Science International, 156*(1), 74–78.

Dyer, A. G., Found, B., & Rogers, D. (2008). An insight into forensic document examiner expertise for discriminating between forged and disguised signatures. *Journal of Forensic Sciences, 53*(5), 1154–1159.

Ediger, M. (2002). Assessing handwriting achievement. *Reading Improvement, 39*(3), 103–111.

Edwards, L. (2003). Writing instruction in kindergarten: Examining an emerging area of research for children with writing and reading difficulties. *Journal of Learning Disabilities, 36*(2), 136–148.

Ellen, D. (2006). *Scientific examination of documents: Methods and techniques.* Boca Raton, FL: CRC Press.

Ezcurra, M. (2012). Terraskin® the paper made from stone: A study of a new writing support for forensic purposes. *Forensic Science International, 220*(1–3), 164–172.

Federal Bureau of Investigation (FBI) (2007). The FBI laboratory report 2007. Retrieved from <http://www.fbi.gov/about-us/lab/lab-annual-report-2007>.

Federal Trade Commission (2001). Electronic signatures in global and national commerce act. (E-SIGN), 15 U.S.C. §§ 7001–7003.

Feinberg, T. E., & Farah, M. J. (Eds.) (1997). *Behavioral neurology and neuropsychology.* New York, NY: McGraw-Hill.

Found, B., & Rogers., D. (1998). A consideration of the theoretical basis of forensic handwriting examination. *International Journal of Forensic Document Examiners, 4*, 109–118.

Found, B., & Rogers, D. (Eds.), (1999). Documentation of forensic handwriting comparison and identification method: A modular approach *Journal of Forensic Document Examination, 12*, 1–68.

Found, B., & Rogers, D. (2003). The initial profiling trial of a program to characterize forensic handwriting examiners' skill. *Journal of the American Society of Questioned Document Examiners, 6*, 72–81.

Found, B., & Rogers, D. (2007). The probative character of forensic document examiners' identification and elimination opinions on questioned signatures. In J. G. Phillips, D. Rogers, & R. P. Ogeil (Eds.), *Proceedings of the thirteenth biennial conference of the International Graphonomics Society*, November 11–14, 2007 (pp. 171–174). Melbourne, Australia: Monash University.

Found, B., Rogers, D., & Herkt, A. (2001). The skill of a group of document examiners in expressing handwriting and signature authorship and production process opinions. *Journal of Forensic Document Examination, 14*, 15–30.

Found, B., Rogers, D., & Metz, H. (1999a). The objective static analysis of spatial errors in simulations. *Journal of Forensic Document Examination, 12*, 81–99.

Found, B., Rogers, D., & Schmittat, R. (1994). A computer program to compare the spatial elements of handwriting. *Forensic Science International, 68*, 195–203.

Found, B., Sita, J., & Rogers, D. (1999b). The development of a program for characterizing forensic handwriting examiners' expertise: Signature examination pilot study. *Journal of Forensic Document Examination, 12*, 69–80.

Franke, K. (2005). *The influence of physical and biomechanical processes on the ink trace: Methodological foundations for the forensic analysis of signatures.* The Netherlands: Artificial Intelligence Institute, University of Groningen (Doctoral dissertation).

Franke, K. (2007a). Dynamic, online signature analysis: Trends and challenges for forensic investigation services. In *Proceedings of seventh international congress of the Gesellschaft für Forensischen Schriftuntersuchung (GFS)*, Salzburg, Austria.

Franke, K. (2007b). Stroke-morphology analysis using super-imposed writing movements. *Computational Forensics: Lecture Notes in Computer Science, 5158/2008*, 204–217.

Franke, K., & Grube, G. (1998). The automatic extraction of pseudodynamic information from static images of handwriting based on marked gray value segmentation. *Journal of Forensic Document Examination, 11*, 17–38.

Franke, K. & Srihari, S. N. (2007). Computational forensics: Towards hybrid-intelligent crime investigation. In *Proceedings of the third international symposium on information assurance and security, IEEE Computer Society*, August 29–31, 2007 (pp. 383–386), Manchester, UK.

Franke, K., Schomaker, L. R. B., Veenhuis, C., Vuurpijl, L. G., van Erp, M., & Guyon, I. (2004). WANDA: A common ground for forensic handwriting examination and writer identification. *ENFHEX News, 1*, 23–47.

Franke, K., Schomaker, L. R. B., Vuurpijl, L. G., & St. Giesler (2003). FISH-new: A common ground for computer-based forensic writer identification. In *Proceedings of the third European Academy of Forensic Science triennial meeting, Istanbul, Turkey, Forensic Science International*, Vol. 136 (Suppl.), 84.

Freeman, F. N. (1918). *The handwriting movement: A study of the motor factors of excellence in penmanship.* Chicago, IL: University of Chicago Press.

Frye v. *United States*, 293F. 1013 (D.C. Cir. 1923).

Gannon Technologies Group (2008). Press Release: Mark Walch, President of Gannon Technology Group, to present at the American Academy of Forensic Sciences annual meeting. Retrieved from <http://www.gannontech.com/press/pr/200801_walch.html>.

Gannon Technologies Group (2011). Biometric handwriting identification: Applications: FLEX-Tracker. Retrieved from <http://www.gannontech.com/data/biometric_applications_tracker.html>.

Gantz, D. T., Miller, J. J., & Walch, M. A. (2005). Multi-language handwriting derived biometric identification. In D. Doermann (Ed.), *Proceedings of the 2005 symposium on document image understanding technology* (pp. 197–209). College Park, Maryland: University of Maryland.

Gervin, M., & Barnes, T. R. E. (2000). Assessment of drug-related movement disorders in schizophrenia. *Advances in Psychiatric Treatment, 6*, 332–343.

Graham, S., & Harris, K. R. (2005). Improving the writing performance of young struggling writers: Theoretical and programmatic research from the center of accelerating student learning. *The Journal of Special Education, 39*(1), 19–33.

Graham, S., Harris, K. R., & Fink, B. (2000). Is handwriting causally related to learning to write? Treatment of handwriting problems in beginning writers. *Journal of Educational Psychology, 92*(1), 620–633.

Graham, S., Weintraub, N., & Berninger, V. (2001). Which manuscript letters to primary grade children write legibly? *Journal of Educational Psychology, 93*(3), 488–497.

Halder-Sinn, P., Enkelmann, C., & Funsch, K. (1998). Handwriting and emotional stress. *Perceptual and Motor Skills, 87*, 457–458.

Halder-Sinn, P., & Funsch, K. (1998). Intra-individual changes in handwriting features depending on handwriting velocity. *Journal of Forensic Document Examination, 11*, 1–16.

Haney, M. R. (2002). Name writing: A window into the emergent literacy skills of young children. *Early Childhood Education Journal, 30*(2), 101–105.

Hardy, H. J. J. (1992). Dynamics of the writing movement: Physical modelling and practical application. *Journal of Forensic Document Examination, 5*, 1–34.

Harralson, H. H. (2005). Handwriting characterization and differential analysis of Parkinson's disease and essential tremor. *Journal of the National Association of Document Examiners, 28*, 19–37.

Harralson, H. H. (2007–2008). Differentiating the handwriting of twins. *Journal of the National Association of Document Examiners, 29*(1), 24–32.

Harralson, H. H. (2010). The NAS report: Implications for forensic document examiners. *Journal of Forensic Document Examination, 20*, 63–70.

Harralson, H. H., Teulings, H. -L., & Farley, B. G. (2008). Comparison of handwriting kinematics in movement disorders and forgery. *Journal of Forensic Document Examination, 19*, 41–52.

Harralson, H. H., Teulings, H.-L., & Farley, B. G. (2009). Handwriting variability in movement disorder patients and effects of fatigue. In A. Vinter & J. -L. Velay (Eds.), *Proceedings of the fourteenth biennial conference of the International Graphonomics Society*, September 13–16, 2009 (pp. 103–107). Dijon, France: Université de Bourgogne.

Harralson, H. H., Teulings, H.-L., & Miller, L. S. (2011). Temporal and spatial differences between online and offline signatures. In E. Grassi & J. L. Contreras-Vidal (Eds.), *Proceedings of the fifteenth International Graphonomics Society conference*, June 12–15, 2011 (pp. 34–37). Cancun, Mexico.

Harrison, W. R. (1958). *Suspect documents*. London: Sweet & Maxwell.

Hermann, W., Eggers, B., Barthel, H., Clark, D., Villmann, T., & Hesse, S., et al. (2002). Correlation between automated writing movements and striatal dopaminergic innervation in patients with Wilson's disease. *Journal of Neurology, 249*, 1082–1087.

Hilton, O. (1993). *Scientific examination of questioned documents*. Boca Raton, FL: CRC Press. Rev. Ed.

Hristova, A. H., & Koller, W. C. (2000). Early Parkinson's disease: What is the best approach to treatment? *Drugs & Aging, 17*(3), 165–181.

Huber, R. A., & Headrick, A. M. (1999). *Handwriting identification: Facts and fundamentals*. Boca Raton, FL: CRC Press.

International Organization for Standardization: ISO/IEC 19794-7 (2007). Information technology—Biometric data interchange formats—Part 7: Signature/sign time series data.

International Organization for Standardization: ISO/IEC 27001 (2005). Information technology—Security techniques—Information security management systems—Requirements.

Isokoski, P., & Käki, M. (2002). Comparison of two touchpad-based methods for numeric entry. In *Proceedings of the SIGCHI conference on human factors in computing systems: changing the world, changing ourselves*, April 20–25, 2002 (pp. 25–32). Minneapolis, MN.

Jain, A. K., Griess, F. D., & Connell, S. D. (2002). On-line signature verification. *Pattern Recognition, 35*(12), 2963–2972.

James, K. H. (2012). How printing practice affects letter perception: An educational cognitive neuroscience perspective. Presented at *Handwriting in the twenty-first century? An educational summit* (January 23, 2012). Washington, DC.

Jindal, D., Kaur, H., & Chattopadhyay, P. K. (1999). A metric analysis of handwriting: A study of signatures. *International Journal of Forensic Document Examiners, 5*, 105–107.

Jones, D., & Christensen, C. A. (1999). Relationship between automaticity in handwriting and students' ability to generate written text. *Journal of Educational Psychology, 91*(1), 44–49.

Joseph, A. B., & Young, R. R. (Eds.) (1992). *Movement disorders in neurology and neuropsychiatry.* Cambridge, MA: Blackwell.

Joseph, R. (1996). *Neuropsychiatry, neuropsychology, and clinical neuroscience* (2nd ed.). Baltimore, MD: Williams & Wilkins.

Kam, M., Fielding, G., & Conn, R. (1997). Writing identification by professional document examiners. *Journal of Forensic Sciences, 42*(5), 778–786.

Kam, M., Gummadidala, K., Fielding, G., & Conn, R. (2001). Signature authentication by forensic document examiners. *Journal of Forensic Sciences, 46*, 884–888.

Kam, M., & Lin, E. (2003). Writer identification using hand-printed and non-hand-printed questioned documents. *Journal of Forensic Sciences, 48*(6), 1391–1395.

Kam, M., Wetstein, J., & Conn, R. (1994). Proficiency of professional document examiners in writer identification. *Journal of Forensic Sciences, 39*(1), 5–14.

Kashi, R. S., Hu, J., Nelson, W. L., & Turin, W. (1997). On-line handwritten signature verification using hidden Markov model features. In *Proceedings of the fourth international conference on document analysis and recognition*, August 18–20, 1997 (pp. 253–257), Ulm, Germany.

KeCrypt Systems Ltd. (2012). Can online signatures be 100% secure? Retrieved from <http://www.security-technologynews.com/article/can-online-signatures-be-100-secure.html>.

Kholmatov, A., & Yanikoglu, B. (2005). Identity authentication using improved online signature verification method. *Pattern Recognition Letters, 26*(15), 2400–2408.

Koller, W., Biary, N., & Cone, S. (1986). Disability in essential tremor: Effect of treatment. *Neurology, 36*, 1001–1004.

Kulvicius, T., Ning, K., Tamosiunaite, M., & Worgötter, F. (2012). Joining movement sequences: Modified dynamic movement primitives for robotics applications exemplified in handwriting. *IEEE Transactions on Robotics, 28*(4), 145–157.

Kumho Tire. Co. v. Carmichael (97-1709). (1999). 131F.3d 1433.

Langmaid, R. A., Papadopoulos, N., Johnson, B. P., Phillips, J. G., & Rinehart, N. J. (2012). Handwriting in children with ADHD. *Journal of Attention Disorders, 16*, 6.

Laszlo, J. I., & Broderick, P. (1991). Drawing and handwriting difficulties: Reasons for and remediation of dysfunction. In J. Wann, A. M. Wing & N. Sovik (Eds.), *Development of graphic skills: Research, perspectives and educational implications.* San Diego, CA: Academic Press.

LaVelle, C. R. (2007). What forensic document examiners should know about digital and electronic signatures. *Journal of Forensic Document Examination, 18*, 63–79.

Leahy, P. (2011). S.132: Criminal justice and forensic science reform act of 2011. Retrieved from <http://www.leahy.senate.gov/press/leahy-proposes-landmark-forensics-reform-legislation>.

Lei, H., & Govindaraju, V. (2005). A comparative study on the consistency of features in on-line signature verification. *Pattern Recognition Letters, 26*(15), 2483–2489.

Leung, S. C., Fung, H. T., Cheng, Y. S., & Poon, N. L. (1993a). Forgery I—simulation. *Journal of Forensic Sciences, 38*(2), 402–412.

Leung, S. C., Fung, H. T., Cheng, Y. S., & Poon, N. L. (1993b). Forgery II—tracing. *Journal of Forensic Sciences, 38*(2), 413–424.

Linderman, M., Lebedev, M. A., & Erlichman, J. S. (2009). Recognition of handwriting from electromyography. *PLoS ONE, 4*(8), e6791. doi 10.1371/journal.pone.000679.

Ling, S. (2002). A preliminary investigation into handwriting examination by multiple measurements of letters and spacing. *Forensic Science International, 126,* 145–149.

Livescribe, Inc. (2012). Smartpen. Retrieved from <http://www.livescribe.com/en-us/smartpen/dotpaper.html>.

Liwicki, M. (2012). Automatic signature verification: In-depth investigation of novel features and different models. *Journal of Forensic Document Examination, 22,* 25–39.

Liwicki, M., van den Heuvel, C. E., Found, B., & Malik, M. I. (2010). Forensic signature verification competition 4NSIGComp2010: Detection of simulated and disguised signatures. In *2010 International conference on frontiers in handwriting recognition (ICFHR)*, November 16–18, 2010 (pp. 715–720).

Longstaff, M. G., & Heath, R. A. (2000). The influence of tremor on handwriting performance under conditions of low and intermediate physical stress. *Journal of Forensic Document Examination, 13,* 25–44.

Longstaff, M. G., & Heath, R. A. (2003). The influence of motor system degradation on the control of handwriting movements: A dynamical systems analysis. *Human Movement Science, 22,* 91–110.

Longstaff, M. G., Mahant, P. R., Stacy, M. A., Van Gemmert, A. W. A., Leis, B. C., & Stelmach, G. E. (2003). Discrete and dynamic scaling of the size of continuous graphic movements of Parkinsonian patients and elderly controls. *Journal of Neurology, Neurosurgery, and Psychiatry, 74,* 299–304.

Lopresti, D. P., & Raim, J. D. (2005). The effectiveness of generative attacks on an online handwriting biometric. In T. Kanade, A. Jain, & N. K. Ratha (Eds.), *Audio- and video-based biometric person authentication, lecture notes in computer science* (Vol. *3546*). Berlin: Springer.

Lou, J. -S., Kearns, G., Oken, B., Sexton, G., & Nutt, J. (2001). Exacerbated physical fatigue and mental fatigue in Parkinson's disease. *Movement Disorders, 16*(2), 190–196.

Lyter, A. H., III (1982). Examination of ball pen ink by high pressure liquid chromatography. *Journal of Forensic Sciences, 27*(1), 154–160.

Lytle, B., & Yang, C. (2006). Detecting forged handwriting with wavelets and statistics. *Rose Hulman Undergraduate Mathematics Journal, 7*(1), 1–10.

Macleod, A. D., & Whitehead, L. E. (1997). Dysgraphia and terminal delirium. *Palliative Medicine, 11,* 127–132.

Maeland, A. F., & Karlsdottir, R. (1991). Development of reading, spelling, and writing skills from third to sixth grade in normal and dysgraphic school children. In J. Wann, A. M. Wing & N. Sovik (Eds.), *Development of graphic skills: Research, perspectives and educational implications*. San Diego, CA: Academic Press.

Marquis, R., Schmittbuhl, M., Mazzella, W. D., & Taroni, F. (2005). Quantification of the shape of handwritten characters: A step to objective discrimination between writers based on the study of the capital character O. *Forensic Science International, 150,* 23–32.

Mason, S. (Ed.) (2010). *Electronic evidence* (2nd ed.). London: Lexis Nexis Butterworths.

Mason, S. (2012). *Electronic signatures in law* (3rd ed.). Cambridge, UK: Cambridge University Press.

Mavrogiorgou, P., Mergl, R., Tigges, P., Husseini, J. E., Schroter, A., & Juckel, G., et al. (2001). Kinematic analysis of handwriting movements in patients with obsessive-compulsive disorder. *Journal of Neurology, Neurosurgery, and Psychiatry, 70*, 605–612.

McBride, H. E. A., & Siegel, L. S. (1997). Learning disabilities and adolescent suicide. *Journal of Learning Disabilities, 30*(6), 652–664.

Mergl, R., Juckel, G., Rihl, J., Henkel, V., Karner, M., & Tigges, P., et al. (2004a). Kinematical analysis of handwriting movements in depressed patients. *Acta Psychiatrica Scandinavica, 109*, 383–391.

Mergl, R., Mavrogiorgou, P., Juckel, G., Zaudig, M., & Hegerl, U. (2004b). Effects of sertraline on kinematic aspects of hand movements in patients with obsessive-compulsive disorder. *Psychopharmacology, 171*, 179–185.

Merlino, M. L., Springer, V., Kelly, J. S., Hammond, D., Sahota, E., & Haines, L. (2007). Meeting the challenges of the Daubert trilogy: Refining and redefining the reliability of forensic evidence. *Tulsa Law Review, 43*(2), 417–445.

Miller, L. S. (1984). Bias among forensic document examiners: A need for procedural changes. *Journal of Police Science and Administration, 12*(4), 407–411.

Miller, L. S. (1987). Procedural bias in forensic examinations of human hair. *Law and Human Behavior, 11*, 157.

Mohammed, L. A., Found, B., Caligiuri, M., & Rogers, D. (2011). The dynamic character of disguise behavior for text-based, mixed, and stylized signatures. *Journal of Forensic Sciences, 56*, 136–141.

Myers, D. G. (2001). *Psychology: Myers in modules* (6th ed.). New York, NY: Worth Publishers.

National Institute of Standards and Technology, (2009). *FIPS PUB 186-3: Digital signature standards (DSS)*. Gaithersburg, MD: Information Technology Laboratory.

National Research Council of the National Academies of Science, (2009). *Strengthening forensic science in the United States: A path forward*. Washington, DC: National Academies Press. (Pre-publication copy)

Nelson, R. H. (2006). *The Peterson method: A research-based strategy for teaching and learning motor skills for written language*. Greensburg, PA: Peterson Directed Handwriting. Retrieved from <http://www.peterson-handwriting.com/Publications/PDF_versions/PetersonStrategy.pdf>.

New York Times (January 26, 2009). The death of handwriting. Retrieved from <http://ideas.blogs.nytimes.com/2009/01/26/the-death-of-handwriting/>.

Niels, R. M. J., & Vuurpijl, L. G. (2005). Using dynamic time warping for intuitive handwriting recognition. In A. Marcelli, & C. de Stefano (Eds.), *Advances in graphonomics: proceedings of the twelfth conference of the International Graphonomics Society*, June 26–29, 2005 (pp. 217–221). Salerno, Italy.

Oliveira, R. M., Gurd, J. M., Nixon, P., Marshall, J. C., & Passingham, R. E. (1997). Micrographia in Parkinson's disease: The effect of providing external cues. *Journal of Neurology, Neurosurgery, and Psychiatry, 63*, 429–433.

Osborn, A. S. (1929). *Questioned documents* (2nd ed.). Albany, NY: Boyd Printing Co..

Pal, P. K., Samii, A., & Calne, D. B. (2002). Cardinal features of early Parkinson's disease. In: W. J. Weiner & S. A. Factor (Eds.), *Parkinson's disease: Diagnosis and medical management*. Medical Publishing, Inc. pp.41–56.

Pepe, A., Rogers, D. K., & Sita, J. C. (2011). A cognitive look into simulations of high and low complexity signatures. In E. Grassi & J. L. Contreras-Vidal (Eds.), *Proceedings of the fifteenth International Graphonomics Society conference*, June 12–15, 2011. Cancun, Mexico.

Pettus v. *United States*. (2012). DCCA 8-CF-1361. Retrieved from <http://legaltimes.typepad.com/files/08-cf-1361_mtd.pdf>.

Peverly, S. (2012). The relationship of transcription speed and other cognitive variables to note-taking and test performance. Presented at *Handwriting in the twenty-first century? An educational summit* (January 23, 2012). Washington, DC. Retrieved from <http://sapersteinassociates.com/data/2_29_HW_Summit_White_Paper_eVersion.pdf>.

Phillips, J. G., Noutsis, S., Hughes, C., & Rogers, D. (2000). Effects of writing speed upon modes of signature simulation: A kinematic analysis. *Journal of Forensic Document Examination, 13,* 1–14.

Phillips, J. G., Ogeil, R. P., & Müller, F. (2009). Alcohol consumption and handwriting: A kinematic analysis. *Human Movement Science, 28*(5), 619–632.

Phillips, J. G., Stelmach, G. E., & Teasdale, N. (1991). What can indices of handwriting quality tell us about Parkinsonian handwriting? *Human Movement Science, 10,* 301–314.

Poulin, G. (1999). The influence of writing fatigue on handwriting characteristics in a selected population part one: General considerations. *International Journal of Forensic Document Examiners, 5,* 193–220.

Provins, K. A., & Magliaro, J. (1989). Skill, strength, handedness, and fatigue. *Journal of Motor Behavior, 21*(2), 113–121.

Reynolds, D. (2008). Gaussian mixture models. *Encyclopedia of Biometric Recognition.* Retrieved from <http://extwebprod.ll.mit.edu/mission/communications/publications/publication-files/full_papers/0802_Reynolds_Biometrics-GMM.pdf>.

Richiardi, J., Fierrez-Aguilar, J., Ortega-Garcia, J., & Drygajlo, A. (2004). On-line signature verification resilience to packet loss in IP networks. In *Proceedings of second COST 275 workshop on biometrics on the internet: fundamentals, advances and applications,* March 2004 (pp. 11–16). Vigo, Spain.

Richiardi, J., Ketabdar, H., & Drygajlo, A. (2005). Local and global feature selection for on-line signature verification. In *International conference on document analysis and recognition,* August 29–September 1, 2005 (pp. 625–629).

Rigoll, G. & Kosmala, A. (1998). A systematic comparison between on-line and off-line methods for signature verification with hidden Markov values. In *Proceedings of the fourteenth international conference on pattern recognition* (pp. 1755–1757).

Risinger, D. M. (2006). Navigating expert reliability: Are criminal standards of certainty being left on the dock? *Albany Law Review, 64,* 99–149.

Risinger, D. M. (2007). Goodbye to all that, or, a fool's errand, by one of the fools: How I stopped worrying about court responses to handwriting identification (and 'Forensic Science' in general) and learned to love misinterpretations of Kumho Tire v. Carmichael. *Tulsa Law Review, 43*(2), 447–475.

Risinger, D. M. (2009). Legal rules for forensic science evidence. In *Proceedings of forensic science for the twenty-first century: The National Academy of Sciences report and beyond conference. Center for the study of law, science, & technology, 3–4 April, 2009, Sandra Day O'Connor College of Law.* Tempe, AZ: Arizona State University.

Samanidou, V. F., Nikolaidou, K. I., & Papadoyannis, I. N. (2007). Development and validation of a gradient–HPLC–PDAD method for the identification of ballpoint pen ink components: Study of their decomposition on aging for forensic science applications. *Journal of Liquid Chromatography & Related Technologies, 27*(2), 215–235.

Saperstein Associates (2012). Handwriting in the twenty-first century? Research shows why handwriting belongs in today's classroom. In *An educational summit* (January 23, 2012). Washington, DC. Retrieved from <http://sapersteinassociates.com/data/2_29_HW_Summit_White_Paper_eVersion.pdf>.

Sarojini, B. K., & Sireesha, K. (2012). A 3-level mapped segmentation based handwriting recognition system. *Special Issue of International Journal of Computer Applications on Advanced Computing and Communication Technologies for HPC Applications (ACCTHPCA)*, *3*, 1–5.

Saudek, R. (1978). *Experiments with handwriting*. Sacramento, CA: Books for Professionals. (Reprint).

Scheidat, T., Vielhaur, C., & Dittmann, J. (2007). Single-semantic, multi-instance fusion of handwriting based biometric authentication systems. In *Proceedings of IEEE international conference on image processing*, September 16–19, 2007 (pp. 393–396), San Antonio, Texas.

Scheidat, T., Wolf, F., & Vielhauer, C. (2006). Analyzing handwriting biometrics in metadata context. In *Proceedings of SPIE*, *6072*, 182–193.

Schirripa Spagnolo, G. (2005). Analysis of handwritten documents by 3D micro-topography. In A. Marcelli & C. De Stefano (Eds.), *Proceedings of the twelfth biennial conference of the International Graphonomics Society, 26–29 June, 2005*, (pp. 242–249), Salerno, Italy.

Schröter, A., Mergl, R., Bürger, K., Hampel, H., Möller, H. -J., & Hegerl, U. (2003). Kinematic analysis of handwriting movements in patients with Alzheimer's disease, mild cognitive impairment, depression and healthy subjects. *Dementia and Geriatric Cognitive Disorders*, *15*(3), 132–142.

Sciacca, E., Langlois-Peter, M. B., Gilhodes, J. C., Margot, P., & Velay, J. L. (2008). The range of handwriting variability under different writing conditions. *Journal of Forensic Document Examination*, *19*, 3–13.

Seaman Kelly, J., & Lindblom, B. S. (2006). *Scientific examination of questioned documents* (2nd ed.). Boca Raton, FL: CRC Press.

Senatore, R., Santoro, A., & Marcelli, A. (2011). From motor to trajectory plan: A feedback loop between unfolding and segmentation to improve writing order recovery. In *Proceedings of the fifteenth conference of the International Graphonomics Society*, June 11–15, 2011. Cancun, Mexico.

Senior, S., Hamed, E., Masoud, M., & Shehata, E. (2012). Characterization and dating of blue ballpoint pen inks using principal component analysis of UV-vis absorption spectra, IR spectroscopy, and HPTLC. *Journal of Forensic Sciences*, *57*(4), 1087–1093.

Siegel, J. A. (2009). Forensic science: Changing from within. In *Proceedings of forensic science for the twenty-first century: The National Academy of Sciences report and beyond conference. Center for the study of law, science, & technology, 3–4 April, 2009, Sandra Day O'Connor College of Law*. Tempe, AZ: Arizona State University.

Silanis Technology, Inc. (2010). Producing persuasive electronic evidence: How to prevent and prepare for legal disputes involving electronic signatures and electronic transactions. Retrieved from <http://www.silanis.com/resource-center/articles-v2/compliance-legal-issues/producing-persuasive-electronic-evidence.html>.

Sita, J., Found, B., & Rogers, D. K. (2002). Forensic handwriting examiners' expertise for signature comparison. *Journal of Forensic Sciences*, *47*(5), 1117–1124.

Sita, J. C., & Rogers, D. (1999). Changes in forgers' handwriting pressure related to the original writer's dynamics. *Journal of Forensic Document Examination*, *12*, 101–112.

Slavin, M. J., Phillips, J. G., Bradshaw, J. L., Hall, K. A., & Presnell, I. (1999). Consistency of handwriting movements in dementia of the Alzheimer's type: A comparison of Huntington's and Parkinson's diseases. *Journal of the International Neuropsychological Society*, *5*(1), 20–25.

Slyter, S. A. (1995). *Forensic signature examination*. Springfield, IL: Charles C. Thomas.

Smith, R. (September 2, 2009). Johnson City police officer fired after forging signatures on citations. <Timesnews.net>. Retrieved from <http://www.timesnews.net/print_article.php?id=9016541>.

SOFTPRO GmbH (2012). Biometric authentication: Leveraging signature biometrics for authentication. Retrieved from <http://www.softpro.de/en/signature-verification/biometric-authentication.aspx>.

Srihari, S. N. (2010). Beyond C.S.I.: The rise of computational forensics. *IEEE Spectrum*, 38–43. Retrieved from <http://spectrum.ieee.org/computing/software/beyond-csi-the-rise-of-computational-forensics/0>.

Srihari, S. N., Cha, S. -H., Arora, H., & Lee, S. (2002). Individuality of handwriting. *Journal of Forensic Sciences*, *47*(4), 1–17.

Srihari, S. N., Huang, C., & Srinivasan, H. (2008). On the discriminability of the handwriting of twins. *Journal of Forensic Sciences*, *53*(2), 430–446.

Stempel-Mathey, L., & Wolf, B. J. (1999). In J. R. Birsh (Ed.), *Multisensory teaching of basic language skills*. Baltimore, MD: Paul H. Brookes Publishing Co.

Strach, S. J. (1998). Probability conclusions in handwriting comparison. *International Journal of Forensic Document Examiners*, *4*(4), 313–317.

Suddath, C. (August 3, 2009). Mourning the death of handwriting. Time Magazine. Retrieved from <http://www.time.com/time/magazine/article/0,9171,1912419,00.html>.

Tariq, S., Sarwar, S., & Hussain, W. (2011). Classification of features into strong and weak features for an intelligent online signature verification system. In *Proceedings of the first international workshop on automated forensic handwriting analysis (AFHA)*, September 17–18, 2011. Beijing, China.

Teulings, H. -L., Contreras-Vidal, J. L., Stelmach, G. E., & Adler, C. H. (1997). Parkinsonism reduces coordination of fingers, wrist, and arm in fine motor control. *Experimental Neurology*, *146*, 159–170.

Teulings, H. -L., Contreras-Vidal, J. L., Stelmach, G. E., & Adler, C. H. (2002). Adaptation of handwriting size under distorted visual feedback in patients with Parkinson's disease and elderly and young controls. *Journal of Neurology, Neurosurgery, and Psychiatry*, *72*, 315–324.

Teulings, H. -L., & Maarse, F. J. (1984). Digital recording and processing of handwriting movements. *Human Movement Science*, *3*, 193–217.

Teulings, H. -L., & Romero, D. H. (2003). Submovement analysis in learning cursive handwriting or block print. In H. -L.Teulings & A. W. A. Van Gemmert (Eds.), *Proceedings of the eleventh conference of the international graphonomics society*, November 2–5, 2003 (pp. 107–110). Scottsdale, Arizona.

Thomassen, A. J. W. M., & Van Galen, G. P. (1997). Temporal features of handwriting: Challenges for forensic analysis. *Journal of Forensic Document Examination*, *10*, 85–104.

Topaz Systems, Inc. (2004). SigCompare signature comparison active-x control. Retrieved from <http://www.topazsystems.com/SigCompare.pdf>.

Topaz Systems, Inc. (2012). Software guidelines. Retrieved from <http://www.topazsystems.com/signaturecapture/guidelines.htm>.

Tucha, O., Aschenbrenner, S., Eichhammer, P., Putzhammer, A., Sartor, H., & Klein, H. E., et al. (2002). The impact of tricyclic antidepressants and selective serotonin reuptake inhibitors on handwriting movements of patients with depression. *Psychopharmacology*, *159*, 211–215.

Tucha, O., & Lange, K. W. (2005). The effect of conscious control on handwriting in children with attention deficit hyperactivity disorder. *Journal of Attention Disorders*, *9*(1), 323–332.

Tucha, O., Walitza, S., Mecklinger, L., Stasik, D., Sontag, T. -A., & Lange, K. W. (2006). The effect of caffeine on handwriting movements in skilled writers. *Human Movement Science*, *25*(4–5), 523–535.

Uitti, R. J.; Baba, Y., Whaley, N. R., Wszolek, Z. K., & Putzke, J. D. (2005). Parkinson disease: Handedness predicts asymmetry. *Neurology*, *4*(11), 1925–1930.

United States v. Starzecpyzel, 880F. Supp. 1027 (S.D.N.Y. 1995).

Van Galen, G. P., & Van Gemmert, A. W. A. (1996). Kinematic and dynamic features of forging another person's handwriting. *Journal of Forensic Document Examination*, *9*, 1–25.

Van Gemmert, A. W. A., Adler, C. H., & Stelmach, G. E. (2003). Parkinson's disease patients undershoot target size in handwriting and similar tasks. *Journal of Neurology, Neurosurgery, and Psychiatry, 74*, 1502–1508.

Van Gemmert, A. W. A., Teulings, H. L., Contreras-Vidal, J. L., & Stelmach, G. E. (1999a). Parkinson's disease and the control of size and speed in handwriting. *Neuropsychologia, 37*, 685–694.

Van Gemmert, A. W. A., Teulings, H. L., & Stelmach, G. E. (1999b). Parkinsonian patients reduce their stroke size in anticipation of increased programming load. In *Proceedings of the ninth biennial conference of the International Graphonomics Society* (pp. 231–236). Singapore: Nanyang Technological University.

Van Gemmert, A. W. A., Teulings, H. L., & Stelmach, G. E. (2001). Parkinsonian patients reduce their stroke size with increased processing demands. *Brain and Cognition, 47*, 504–512.

Van Gemmert, A. W. A., & Van Galen, G. P. (1996). Dynamic features of mimicking another person's writing and signature. In M. L. Simner, C. G. Leedham & A. J. W. M. Thomassen (Eds.), *Handwriting and drawing research: Basic and applied issues* (pp. 459–471). Amsterdam: IOS Press.

Walch, M. A., & Gantz, D. T. (2004). Pictographic-matching: A graph-based approach towards a language independent document exploitation platform. In *Proceedings of the first ACM workshop on hardcopy document processing*, November 8–13, 2004 (pp. 53–64). Washington, DC.

Walters, A. S., & Hening, W. A. (1992). Noise-induced psychogenic tremor associated with post-traumatic stress disorder. *Movement Disorders, 7*(4), 333–338.

Werner, P., Rosenblum, S., Bar-On, G., Heinik, J., & Korczyn, A. (2006). Handwriting process variables discriminating mild Alzheimer's disease and mild cognitive impairment. *The Journals of Gerontology, 61*(4), 228–236.

Will, E. (2012). Inferring relative speed of handwriting from the static trace. *Journal of Forensic Document Examination, 22*, 55–63.

Witswell Consulting & Services, Inc. (2009). Cyber-SIGN biometric signature authentication. Retrieved from <http://www.cybersign.com/com/CSIacrobat.html>.

WonderNet, Ltd. (N.D.). Paper-free digital signature solutions. Retrieved from <http://www.penflow.com/index.php?option=com_content&task=view&id=36&Itemid=45>.

Yan, J. H., Rountree, S., Massman, P., Smith Doody, R., & Li, H. (2008). Alzheimer's disease and mild cognitive impairment deteriorate fine movement control. *Journal of Psychiatric Research, 42*(14), 1203–1212.

Zhang, Y., Shi, G., & Yang, J. (2009). HMM-based online recognition of handwritten chemical symbols. In *Tenth international conference on document analysis and recognition (ICDAR)*, July 26–29, 2009 (pp. 1255–1259).

Zimmerman, J. (1998). Counting handwriting characteristics. *International Journal of Forensic Document Examiners, 4*(4), 318–322.

CPSIA information can be obtained at www.ICGtesting.com
Printed in the USA
BVOW04s0710041113

335312BV00013B/87/P